**Report by the
Comptroller and Auditor General**

Protecting the Financial Welfare of People with Mental Incapacity

Ordered by the
House of Commons
to be printed 9 February 1999

Anthony Spires
May 1999

LONDON: The Stationery Office

£13.10

HC 206 Session 1998–99
Published 12 February 1999

This report has been prepared under Section 6 of the National Audit Act 1983 for presentation to the House of Commons in accordance with Section 9 of the Act.

John Bourn
Comptroller and Auditor General

National Audit Office
29 January 1999

The Comptroller and Auditor General is the head of the National Audit Office employing some 750 staff. He, and the National Audit Office, are totally independent of Government. He certifies the accounts of all Government departments and a wide range of other public sector bodies; and he has statutory authority to report to Parliament on the economy, efficiency and effectiveness with which departments and other bodies have used their resources.

For further information about the National Audit Office please contact:

National Audit Office
Press Office
157-197 Buckingham Palace Road
Victoria
London
SW1W 9SP

Tel: 0171-798 7400

email:nao@gtnet.gov.uk

Web site address: http://www.open.gov.uk/nao/home.htm

Contents

Figure 1

Procedures leading to the appointment of a receiver for a person with mental incapacity

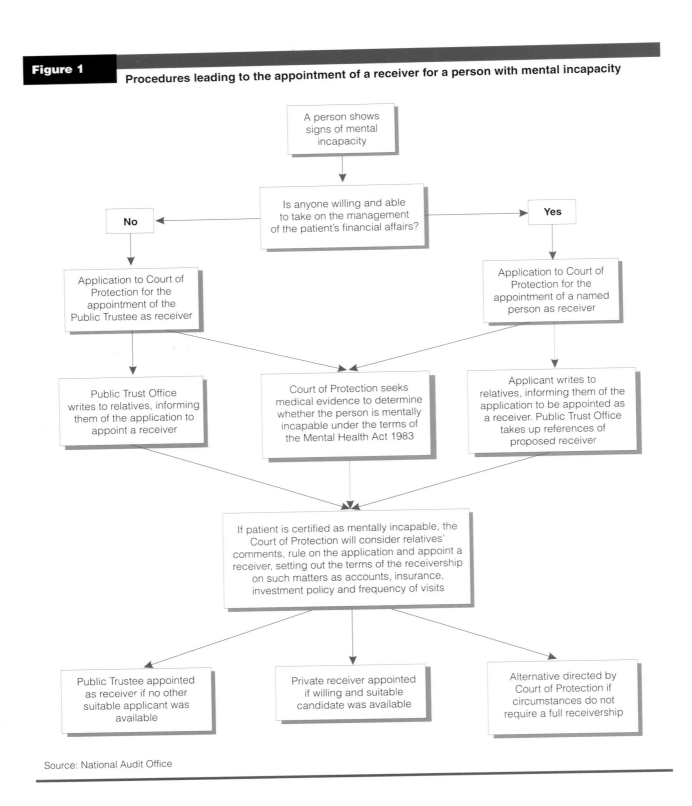

Source: National Audit Office

Executive summary

1   When a person becomes mentally incapable of handling their own affairs it may be necessary for the Court of Protection to appoint a receiver to look after their day to day finances, such as receiving benefits and paying bills (Figure 1). The application to the Court to appoint a receiver may be made by anyone concerned about the finances of a mentally incapable person. Any person can be considered by the Court to be appointed as receiver, but it most frequently appoints relatives of the "patient", solicitors or local authorities; these are known as private receiverships. Where no one is willing or able to act as receiver, the Public Trustee – the Chief Executive of the Public Trust Office – may be appointed to act directly on the patient's behalf; these are known as Public Trustee receiverships (paragraphs 1.1 to 1.2).

2   The Public Trust Office, an executive agency within the Lord Chancellor's Department, is responsible for the administration of all cases under the Court of Protection's jurisdiction. It currently administers or supervises some 22,000 receiverships, including around 2,500 Public Trustee receiverships. The Public Trust Office controls patients' capital assets worth some £1.45 billion and supervises or manages their investments. It charges patients fees to recover the cost of its monitoring and receivership work, currently around £11.5 million a year (paragraphs 1.3 to 1.6).

3   We reported on the work of the Public Trust Office in 1994, and the Committee of Public Accounts subsequently made a number of recommendations for improvement. This report examines progress since then.

Main findings

Monitoring receivers

4   Receivers appointed by the Court of Protection have discretion in spending the income of the patients for whom they act. The Court requires them to account for all money received and paid out on behalf of the patient, normally on an annual basis. We found that where receivers were submitting accounts they were generally of a good quality. However, many receivers do not meet the requirement to submit accounts on a regular basis. Our examination found that almost 40 per cent of receivers had not submitted an account during 1996-97 (paragraphs 2.2 to 2.3, 2.5 and 2.14).

5   The Court of Protection, after considering patients' individual circumstances, insists in the majority of cases, approximately two-thirds, that the receivers arrange insurance against misappropriation of patients' funds. Of the cases in our sample where there were either no accounts or accounts outstanding for more than one year, two-thirds did not have insurance. Although the individual circumstances of some of these patients may not originally have justified insurance, we believe that the absence of both accounts and insurance may put some patients' assets at particular risk (paragraphs 2.10 to 2.12).

6   We found that the Public Trust Office's review of accounts was thorough, but the timeliness of review had deteriorated since 1994, when it made a commitment to the Committee of Public Accounts to review 80 per cent of private receivership accounts within four weeks of receipt and 80 per cent of Public Trustee receivership accounts within eight weeks. Around one quarter of the private receivers' accounts in our sample had been reviewed within four weeks of receipt. Taking account of sampling error, this gives a range of 16 to 34 per cent for actual performance, compared with the target of 80 per cent, and with 85 per cent for accounts submitted in 1992-93, which were considered in our previous report. In the case of Public Trustee receiverships, accounts are prepared by the cashier and reviewed by a separate part of the Public Trust Office. Only one-third of Public Trustee accounts in our sample had been reviewed within eight weeks, against 53 per cent in 1992-93 (paragraphs 2.15 to 2.19 and 2.29).

7   The Public Trust Office, on behalf of the Court of Protection, initially classifies private receivers as high, medium or low risk, partly on the basis of the receiver's family relationship with the patient. Subsequent assessments of risk are made during the review of the receiver's annual account, for example to reflect any major change in the patient's circumstances. Whilst the Public Trust Office called in only 13 insurance bonds in 1997 out of the 13,000 held, we believe that there is insufficient information on the activities of receivers who fail to submit accounts to judge the possible level of undetected abuse (paragraphs 2.11 and 2.23 to 2.25).

Visiting patients

8   Visits to patients provide an opportunity for feed-back on how well a receivership is operating and can alert the Public Trust Office to any action required to ensure that the needs of patients are properly and promptly addressed. Visitors do not have any responsibility to review patients' financial affairs. Where the Public Trustee acts as receiver, the aim is to visit all patients at least once a year. Only 67 per cent of such patients were visited during 1996-97, against 86 per cent in 1992-93, in part because one visitor was on long-term sickness absence (paragraphs 3.1 and 3.7).

9 Until November 1998, visits were made to private receivership patients not excluded by criteria set by the Court of Protection in 1988, and the Public Trust Office believes that every year it visits all such patients who require visits. Since our last report in 1994, the Public Trust Office has taken responsibility from the Lord Chancellor's Department for visits to private receivership patients and has appointed six specialist visitors, allowing it to carry out a maximum of 2,000 visits a year within existing funds. In 1997-98 the Public Trust Office made 1,680 visits to patients, just over ten per cent more than in 1992-93 when the Committee of Public Accounts considered the level of visits (1,500) to be unacceptably low. The 1992-93 level was however higher than usual because the Public Trust Office committed extra resources to tackling a developing backlog. The 1,680 visits carried out in 1997-98 were double the level of around 800 completed both in 1994-95 and 1995-96. There have been efficiency savings of about £140 per visit (paragraphs 3.4, 3.8 and 3.11).

10 The Public Trust Office currently records information on visits manually. It does not collate data on the characteristics of the patients visited, the recommendations made by visitors or the action it has taken as a result of a visit. Such information would help inform the strategic management of visits. In 1998 the Public Trust Office proposed, and the Court agreed to, changes in the 1988 criteria for patient visits; by November 1998 these changes had been implemented. The Public Trust Office told us that within both the previous and the new criteria there is no discretion for it specifically to target visits towards, for example, patients whose receivers have failed to submit accounts (paragraphs 3.9 and 3.15).

Managing patients' capital

11 The Public Trust Office supervises the investment of over £1.45 billion of patients' capital. In 1994, the Committee of Public Accounts recommended that patients' investment requirements should be subject to annual review. This is generally done at the same time as receivers' accounts are reviewed. However, as many accounts are not submitted or are submitted late, the investment requirements of many patients, some with substantial portfolios, are not subject to annual or prompt review. The Public Trust Office told us that in its experience it is sufficient for caseworkers to consider the need for a review of the investment requirement when they receive information on a material change in the patient's circumstances (paragraphs 4.1 to 4.5).

12   The Public Trust Office invests just under half of all patients' capital in an interest-bearing deposit account managed by the National Debt Commissioners. We found that since 1994 patients have received a return two to three per cent higher than that produced by the Public Trust Office's model, which is based on a set of high street comparators (paragraphs 4.6 and 4.19).

13   Where a patient's assets exceed £150,000, the Public Trust Office generally arranges for capital to be invested in a segregated portfolio which will include a spread of individual securities. An independent committee of financial experts, the Honorary Investment Advisory Committee, advises on the overall investment strategy, and two city brokers appointed by the Public Trust Office manage 84 per cent of the portfolios invested on behalf of private receivership patients. Independent brokers manage the remaining 16 per cent. The brokers receive a commission which is charged against transactions carried out on behalf of the patients. The Public Trust Office told us that the services provided by the brokers would normally only be available from advisors on a management fee basis, which would be considerably more expensive. For the 900 portfolios invested on behalf of Public Trustee patients, the Public Trust Office's own staff make the investment decisions (paragraphs 4.7 to 4.11).

14   Since 1994, the Public Trust Office's one-year investment performance target has been that 85 per cent of patients' portfolios should perform within at least 5 per cent of an appropriately weighted index of recognised market measures. The target assesses the capital performance of portfolios, not income earned on investments. In 1995-96 and 1996-97 the target was missed by two and a half per cent and two per cent respectively. A target for longer term growth (three years) was introduced in 1996-97 with the aim of ensuring that 80 per cent of portfolios achieved capital growth of at least 95 per cent of the weighted index. Only 72 per cent of portfolios met this target in 1996-97. Performance against both targets further deteriorated in 1997-98 to 67 per cent and 47 per cent respectively for the one-year and three-year targets (Figure 16, paragraphs 4.13, 4.15 and 4.20 to 4.21).

15   The Public Trust Office told us that these disappointing performance figures were primarily the result of exceptional growth in particular stockmarket sectors, which were hard to match for long-term diversified portfolios consistent with the investment approach approved by the Court of Protection. It pointed out that even portfolios which did not reach the Public Trust Office's target performance still provided capital appreciation for patients which exceeded inflation (paragraph 4.22).

16 In 1996, the Public Trust Office found that the performance against the one and three-year capital targets of one of its brokers – James Capel Investment Management – was substantially below that of the other broker and the Public Trust Office's own investment staff, and was the main reason for the failure to meet these targets. In conjunction with the Honorary Investment Advisory Committee, it explored with the broker the reasons for the relative under-performance against the targets, and agreed to the restructuring of certain patients' portfolios. However, the Public Trust Office judged that there had been a further deterioration in capital performance and administration, and in November 1997 it gave the company notice that its contract would be terminated on 20 March 1998. In arriving at this decision, the Public Trust Office sought the advice of the Honorary Investment Advisory Committee, and took into account stockmarket movements in the previous three years and the relative performance of the other broker against the capital targets (paragraphs 4.26 to 4.30 and 4.33).

17 The overall financial impact on patients of James Capel Investment Management's performance against the one and three-year capital targets is not known. The Public Trust Office does not collate global information on capital growth with investment income, but follows the capital-only performance standard published by the Association of Private Client Investment Managers and Stockbrokers. It also takes the view that the prime aim of the performance assessment is to assess achievement at the individual fund level, taking into account the patient's circumstances. It considered that since the broker had already reported the income and capital growth individually to each receiver, further monitoring information would be inconclusive and would involve unnecessary expense for patients (paragraphs 4.15 and 4.27).

18 The Public Trust Office does not believe that the one and three-year indicators based largely on the performance of these brokers are an appropriate measure of its own performance, although it remains responsible to the Court of Protection for securing the effective investment of patients' funds. It recently announced their replacement with a new target, which records whether the responsible broker has reviewed the patient's investment portfolio at least once within a 12-month period rather than measuring the level of investment performance achieved. The Public Trust Office will continue to monitor brokers' performance against the one and three-year targets and the results will be disclosed to patients' receivers, the Court of Protection and the Honorary Investment Advisory Committee. The results will continue to be published in the Public Trust Office's Annual Report (paragraphs 4.16 to 4.17).

Financial management

19 The Public Trust Office was established as an executive agency on 1 July 1994 and originally aimed to produce auditable, commercial style financial statements from 1996-97, but will not now do so until 1998-99 because of weaknesses in its accounting policies, systems and procedures (paragraphs 5.3 to 5.7).

20 The Public Trust Office's accounting policy for annual fees is to recognise them in full in the year in which they are raised, and to recognise fee adjustments in the year in which they are made. The Public Trust Office considers that the policy applied ensures that there is a sufficiently close relationship between fee income and expenditure overall. However, generally accepted accounting practice requires that income should be matched to the period of the administration of patients' cases by financial year. Based on an extrapolation of sample case results, we estimate that around £4.6 million of accrued income was therefore excluded from the balance sheet at 31 March 1997. There is no estimate for the equivalent accrued income at 1 April 1996 which, if shown, the Public Trust Office considers would be of a broadly similar amount. The Public Trust Office is now in the process of revising the accounting policy so that it will be able to derive the benefits of the more demanding commercial style of accounting expected of an executive agency (paragraphs 5.22 to 5.24).

21 We found that the Public Trust Office had particular problems in recording, collecting and accounting for fee income from receiverships on a timely and accurate basis. Fees are levied on an estimated basis annually in arrears until they are verified using the income detail from the receivers' accounts, and therefore adjustments will often be required to either collect or refund the differences. The late or non-submission of patients' accounts may adversely affect the final calculation of the annual fee as does the failure to adjust fee levels accurately where necessary following review of accounts. We found that 31 per cent of private receivership fees and 42 per cent of Public Trustee receivership fees due in 1996-97 had not been recorded correctly in the accounting records. Our statistical evaluation of the results of a sample of private receivership cases concluded that errors of understatements and overstatements amounted to some £1.3 million (gross) compared to the total of £8.7 million recorded for this source of income. Although both types of error together resulted in negligible overall monetary impact, they distorted the information available to management (paragraphs 5.11 to 5.18).

22 Our sample review indicates that it took the Public Trust Office more than seven months on average to complete fee collection procedures, although in part this reflects its approach of reviewing some Public Trustee receivership cases every two years in accordance with the risk associated with them. Some £2.7 million in fees due prior to 1996-97 has been identified by the Public Trust Office as uncollected in previous years. Although around £2.4 million of these fees were received in 1996-97, procedures to identify outstanding amounts were incomplete and it is likely that additional debts have yet to be identified (paragraphs 5.19 to 5.21).

23 The Public Trust Office's year end accounting procedures were not sufficiently robust and, as a consequence, material expenditure items (overstatements and understatements) have been included in the wrong year of account. Overall the Public Trust Office was not in a position to produce robust financial data. The uncertainties about the accuracy of recorded information means that only limited reliance can be placed on the data contained in the published 1996-97 financial statements (paragraphs 5.9 and 5.25 to 5.26).

24 The Public Trust Office has reported that it met its targets for efficiency savings agreed with the Lord Chancellor's Department for each of the three financial years 1994 to 1997. We have concluded that in the absence of independently audited accounts, there can be only limited assurance that the available financial statements provide consistent information on which to assess financial performance or that the amounts included are materially accurate. It is therefore not possible to confirm that these targets were actually achieved or that the Public Trust Office met the commitment it gave to the Committee of Public Accounts in 1994 to reduce unit costs by at least two per cent in real terms for each of the next three years (paragraphs 5.8, 5.10 and 5.27 to 5.29).

25 Ministers have approved the subsidy of Public Trustee receivership patients from fees charged to private receivership patients. Reducing the cross subsidy to zero was considered to be an unacceptable additional expense to Public Trustee receivership patients whose cases require more intense management and therefore involve greater cost. The Public Trust Office reduced the subsidy of Public Trustee receiverships by private receiverships from 52 per cent at the time of our last report in 1994 to 37 per cent in 1996-97, against a commitment to the Committee of Public Accounts to achieve 30 per cent by that date. The Public Trust Office largely achieved this reduction by lowering the fees charged to most patients with private receivers, and increasing the fees charged to Public Trustee receivership patients to an average of 21 per cent of the patient's income after deductions. In 1997-98, the subsidy was further reduced to 32 per cent (paragraphs 5.33 to 5.36).

Customer service

26 The Public Trust Office has made progress since 1994 in improving customer care and its surveys of receivers have found rising levels of satisfaction with the service provided. The organisations we consulted confirmed this view. Even so, in 1996-97 the Public Trust Office achieved only five of the 22 target standards it has set itself for dealing with receiverships. In each of the three financial years 1994 to 1997 it has fallen slightly below its overall target for measuring service against standards. This overall indicator does not, however, provide a meaningful picture of performance, since it aggregates different elements of service into a single measure and does not weight the relative importance of each individual service to customers. In 1998, the Public Trust Office surveyed clients on the importance they place on its individual service standards and is currently analysing the results (paragraphs 6.2 to 6.6, 6.10 and 6.20).

Recommendations

27 Since we last reported, there is evidence of increased satisfaction with the service provided by the Public Trust Office. However, there are still weaknesses in its monitoring of receivers' use of patients' money and in the information available to enable decisions to be taken on repeat visits. Accountability is impaired by weaknesses in performance measurement and lack of progress in developing accurate and consistent executive agency accounts.

28 Appendix 1 lists 27 recommendations for improving performance in the handling of the financial affairs of people with mental incapacity. The Public Trust Office should take action on these as a matter of urgency, consulting with the Court of Protection and Lord Chancellor's Department where appropriate.

29 In summary, the priority areas of action for the Public Trust Office are to:

on monitoring receivers

- ensure that late accounts are pursued vigorously by caseworkers with periodic mandatory review by line managers; consider the need for enforceable sanctions against receivers who repeatedly fail to submit accounts promptly; and ensure that patients' funds are adequately protected by insurance bonds.

■ promptly review private and Public Trustee receivership accounts so that effective and timely use can be made of the results of the review; and develop a risk assessment approach to reviewing private receivership accounts, accompanied by greater delegation of authority to receivers classed as low risk.

on visiting patients

■ ensure, unless exceptional circumstances exist, that all Public Trustee receivership patients receive an annual visit.

■ improve management information on whether visit requirements for individual patients are being met.

■ investigate the reasons for the wide differences in the proportion of visits to patients across regions; assess the adequacy of arrangements for returning patients to the visit list once they are removed and ensure that repeat visits are concentrated on patients with the greatest need.

on managing patients' capital

■ ensure that there is a sufficiently robust system in place for monitoring panel brokers which would prompt early and effective action where there is evidence of poor performance.

on financial management

■ draw up an action plan detailing the resources required to review all fee accounts, establish material accruals, and a timetable for the production of auditable accounts for 1998-99, so that management decisions can be taken on the basis of audited financial information.

■ ensure that fee adjustments and errors in fee calculations are identified and addressed promptly; establish and implement a comprehensive income policy to cover the raising, recording, review and collection of fee income from receivership patients; and apply appropriate accounting treatment to all material transactions.

on customer service

■ consult with customers to identify which of the standards relating to receiverships are the most important to them and publish annual performance against these standards.

30 Following a Law Commission review of all types of decision-making on behalf of mentally incapacitated adults, the Government published the Green Paper "Who Decides?" in December 1997. The Law Commission highlighted the likely rise in the numbers of mentally incapacitated adults suffering from dementia as the population aged 80 and over continues to rise, and the growing concern about the potential financial abuse of such vulnerable people.

31 The Green Paper accepted that current law does not always offer sufficient protection either for mentally incapacitated adults or for those who look after them. There was, therefore, a need to reform the law in order to improve and clarify the decision-making process for those who are unable to make decisions for themselves. If implemented, the changes proposed by the Law Commission and reflected in the Government's Green Paper would have significant implications for the future role and duties of the Public Trust Office, since they envisage new responsibilities for the Court of Protection, including a direct interest in healthcare and personal welfare. The observations, conclusions and recommendations made in this report are pertinent to the Government's consultation.

Part 1: Introduction

Role of the Court of Protection

1.1 Mental incapacity afflicts a wide range of people from the very young to the very old and with widely varying degrees of severity. Some of these people may be highly dependent on nursing care, for example, a patient in a psychogeriatric ward, whilst others may live in their own home, do their own shopping and have gainful employment. But they may all be unable to appreciate the importance of money or make appropriate financial plans. Mental incapacity can restrict a person's ability to deal with money, receive pensions or buy or sell property, making them susceptible to exploitation or even fraud. A person may only legally act on their behalf if they have been appointed to do so by the Court of Protection.

1.2 The function of the Court of Protection is to protect and control the administration and affairs of persons in England and Wales who, through mental disorder, are incapable of managing their financial affairs. Under the Mental Health Act 1983, the Court has the authority to appoint an individual or an organisation such as a local authority to administer the financial affairs of a mentally incapacitated person (Case 1). In a minority of cases, where no one else is willing, able or suitable, the Court may appoint the Chief Executive of the Public Trust Office, the Public Trustee, as "receiver of last resort" (Case 2).

A patient for whom a private person acts as receiver (a private receivership)

Case 1

Mr A, now in his twenties, sustained serious brain injuries in a road traffic accident as a child and is incapable of looking after his own financial affairs. In 1986 he was awarded around £200,000 in a court settlement following the accident. His parents did not wish to take on the duties of a receivership so a solicitor was appointed as receiver. The patient has an assessable annual income of £10,000 and pays an annual administration fee of £765 to the Public Trust Office. He also incurs the costs of the solicitor acting as receiver.

A patient for whom the Public Trustee acts as receiver (a Public Trustee receivership)

Case 2

Mr B, an 84 year-old paranoid schizophrenic, was admitted to a residential home in 1993 after living on the streets for four years. He has no known relatives. The Public Trustee was appointed receiver in 1995. Mr B has an assessable annual income of £4,000 and pays a fee of £800 to the Public Trust Office to cover the receivership and annual administration.

1.3 The Court of Protection currently oversees 22,000 receiverships for patients certified by a doctor as mentally incapable under the terms of the Mental Health Act 1983, comprising around 19,500 private receiverships and 2,500 Public Trustee receiverships. It also handles some 6,500 applications to have a receiver appointed and the administration involved in winding up 8,000 receiverships, as well as processing some 10,000 applications each year to register an Enduring Power of Attorney. The roles and responsibilities relating to both private receiverships and to Public Trustee receiverships are outlined in Figure 2 opposite. Over 60 per cent of patients live in private nursing homes or in National Health Service accommodation. More than two-thirds are over 65 years old and a large majority of these older patients are women (Figure 3).

Age and gender of persons whose financial affairs are administered through the Court of Protection

Figure 3

Over two-thirds of all patients are over 65 years old and a large majority of these older patients are women.

Age of Patients

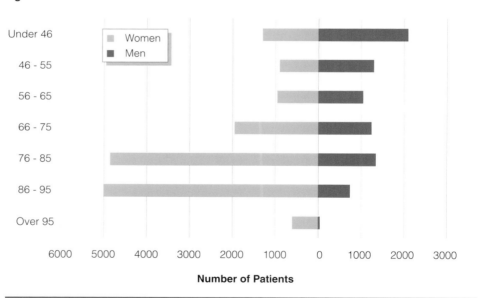

Source: Public Trust Office

Number of Patients

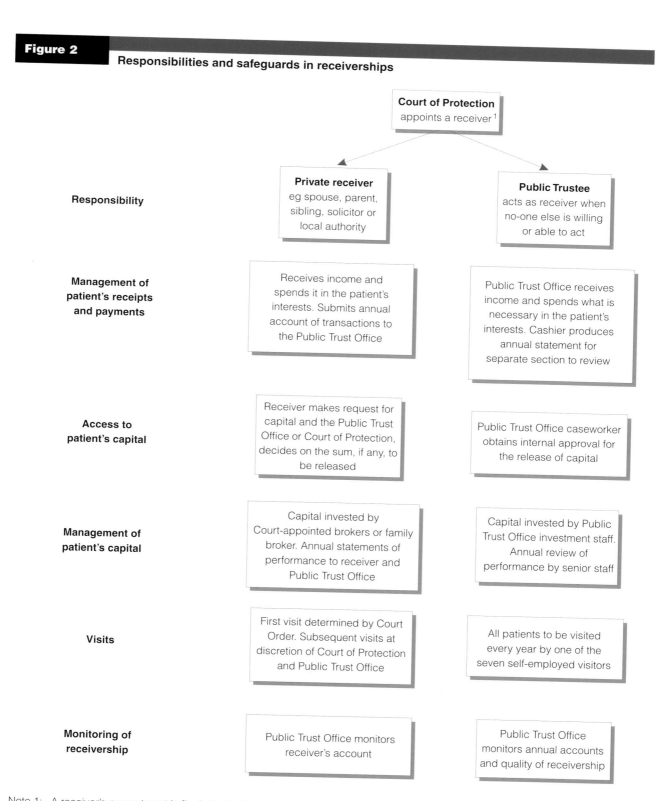

Figure 2

Responsibilities and safeguards in receiverships

Court of Protection
appoints a receiver [1]

| Responsibility | **Private receiver**
eg spouse, parent, sibling, solicitor or local authority | **Public Trustee**
acts as receiver when no-one else is willing or able to act |
|---|---|---|
| **Management of patient's receipts and payments** | Receives income and spends it in the patient's interests. Submits annual account of transactions to the Public Trust Office | Public Trust Office receives income and spends what is necessary in the patient's interests. Cashier produces annual statement for separate section to review |
| **Access to patient's capital** | Receiver makes request for capital and the Public Trust Office or Court of Protection, decides on the sum, if any, to be released | Public Trust Office caseworker obtains internal approval for the release of capital |
| **Management of patient's capital** | Capital invested by Court-appointed brokers or family broker. Annual statements of performance to receiver and Public Trust Office | Capital invested by Public Trust Office investment staff. Annual review of performance by senior staff |
| **Visits** | First visit determined by Court Order. Subsequent visits at discretion of Court of Protection and Public Trust Office | All patients to be visited every year by one of the seven self-employed visitors |
| **Monitoring of receivership** | Public Trust Office monitors receiver's account | Public Trust Office monitors annual accounts and quality of receivership |

Note 1:   A receiver's power to act is firmly limited to the terms of the Court of Protection's order setting up the receivership

Source: National Audit Office analysis of Public Trust Office procedures

1.4   The Court of Protection requires medical evidence that a person is mentally incapable before appointing someone to manage their financial affairs. The person then appointed may well be the same person who applied to the Court to have a receiver appointed. Figure 4 shows that more than half of receivers are relatives. Where there are others of a nearer or equal degree of kinship to the patient, the applicant to the Court is required to inform them about the application to allow them the opportunity to lodge an objection. The Court will consider any objections in deciding whether to make a receivership and who the receiver should be, and will require a reference from a referee who has known the proposed receiver for at least two years (Figure 1).

Who are the receivers?   **Figure 4**

About half of all receivers appointed are related to the patient. Solicitors and local authorities also act as receivers. For 11 per cent of applications the Public Trustee is appointed.

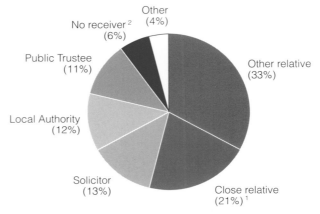

Notes: 1 Close relatives are spouse, parent or child of the mentally incapable person

2 Where a person's assets are modest and straightforward they may be dealt with without the appointment of a receiver

Source: Public Trust Office

Role of the Public Trust Office

1.5   The Court of Protection's judicial decisions are put into effect and managed by the Public Trust Office. Its aim is to ensure the effective management of the private assets and financial affairs of the patients. It employs 570 staff and had a gross budget of £19.5 million in 1996-97. The organisational structure of the Public Trust Office is set out at Figure 5. Its Mental Health Sector takes the lead on receivership work which impacts on the well-being of around 22,000 people with mental incapacity, with assets totalling some £1.45 billion. Another 14,000 people have cases at various stages of administration within the Public Trust Office

**Organisation of the
Public Trust Office**

Figure 5

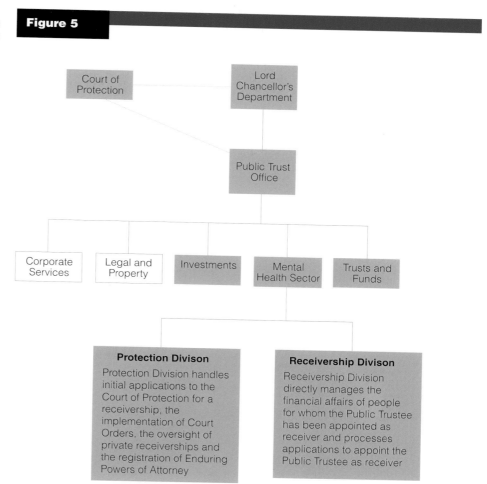

Note: Receiverships are primarily the responsibility of the Mental Health Sector but other divisions
are consulted as necessary. From May 1998 the Head of Trusts and Funds assumed
responsibility for producing the agency's financial statements.

Source: Public Trust Office

involving, for example, the application for, or discharge of, a receivership. Private
receivership and Public Trustee receivership caseloads have grown by 16 per cent
and 4 per cent respectively since 1993-94, and are projected to grow further.

1.6   Within the Mental Health Sector of the Public Trust Office, Protection
Division supervises private receivers and the Receivership Division manages cases
where the Public Trustee has been appointed as receiver. Protection Division is
also responsible for registering Enduring Powers of Attorney, a legal instrument by
which a person can grant a nominee authority to deal with their financial affairs.
On behalf of the Court of Protection, the Public Trust Office retains control over the
capital assets of all patients and directly manages or supervises their investments.
It charges each patient an annual fee for either the support and oversight of the

patient's private receiver, or for the direct management of the receivership where the Public Trustee has been appointed. Fees are set at a level to recover the full costs of monitoring and administering receiverships, currently around £11.5 million a year.

1.7   Other people and organisations may be involved in the care and support of a person with mental incapacity (Figure 6). Along with the Public Trust Office, they aim to meet patients' medical, personal welfare and financial needs in a variety of official, voluntary and personal relationships with patients.

Previous examinations

1.8   We previously examined the Public Trust Office in 1994 in our report *"Looking after the Financial Affairs of People with Mental Incapacity" (HC 258, 1993-94).* In its subsequent report in July 1994 (Thirty-ninth Report of 1993-94), the Committee of Public Accounts made recommendations for improvements in the following areas:

- support of receivers;

- the scrutiny of receivers' annual accounts;

- the level of visits to patients;

- the quality of service provided to clients;

- the level of fees charged; and

- the cross subsidy of Public Trustee patients by private receivership patients.

The recommendations made by the Committee of Public Accounts are detailed in Appendix 2. The Committee expressed a wish to review the Public Trust Office's progress in two to three years' time.

Figure 6

People and organisations involved in the care and support of people with mental incapacity

Court of Protection

Makes initial decisions about who should administer the property and affairs of a person coming under its jurisdiction and how that administration should take effect. Also takes day to day decisions about certain matters such as the disposal of property and gifts made from the patient's assets.

Receiver

Manages patient's income and expenditure. Required to produce annual account for review by Public Trust Office.[1]

Public Trust Office Caseworker

Monitors the receiver to ensure the patient's financial needs are being met. Assesses patient's investment needs. Manages administration on behalf of the Court of Protection.

Carer

Attends to patient's physical and other needs. May also be the receiver.

Public Trust Office Visitor

Visits the patient to ascertain whether needs are being met and that the receivership is working properly. Need for visits decided initially by the Court of Protection.

Patient with mental incapacity

Solicitor

May assist receiver in seeking appointment by the Court of Protection and in managing the patient's finances. Acts as receiver for 13 per cent of patients.

Benefits Agency

Pays Income Support, Disability Living Allowance, Housing Benefit where applicable.

Local Authority Social Services

May provide services such as personal assistance, meals on wheels or accommodation, according to the patient's needs. Acts as receiver in 12 per cent of cases.

National Health Service

A qualified medical practitioner must certify that the person is mentally incapable.

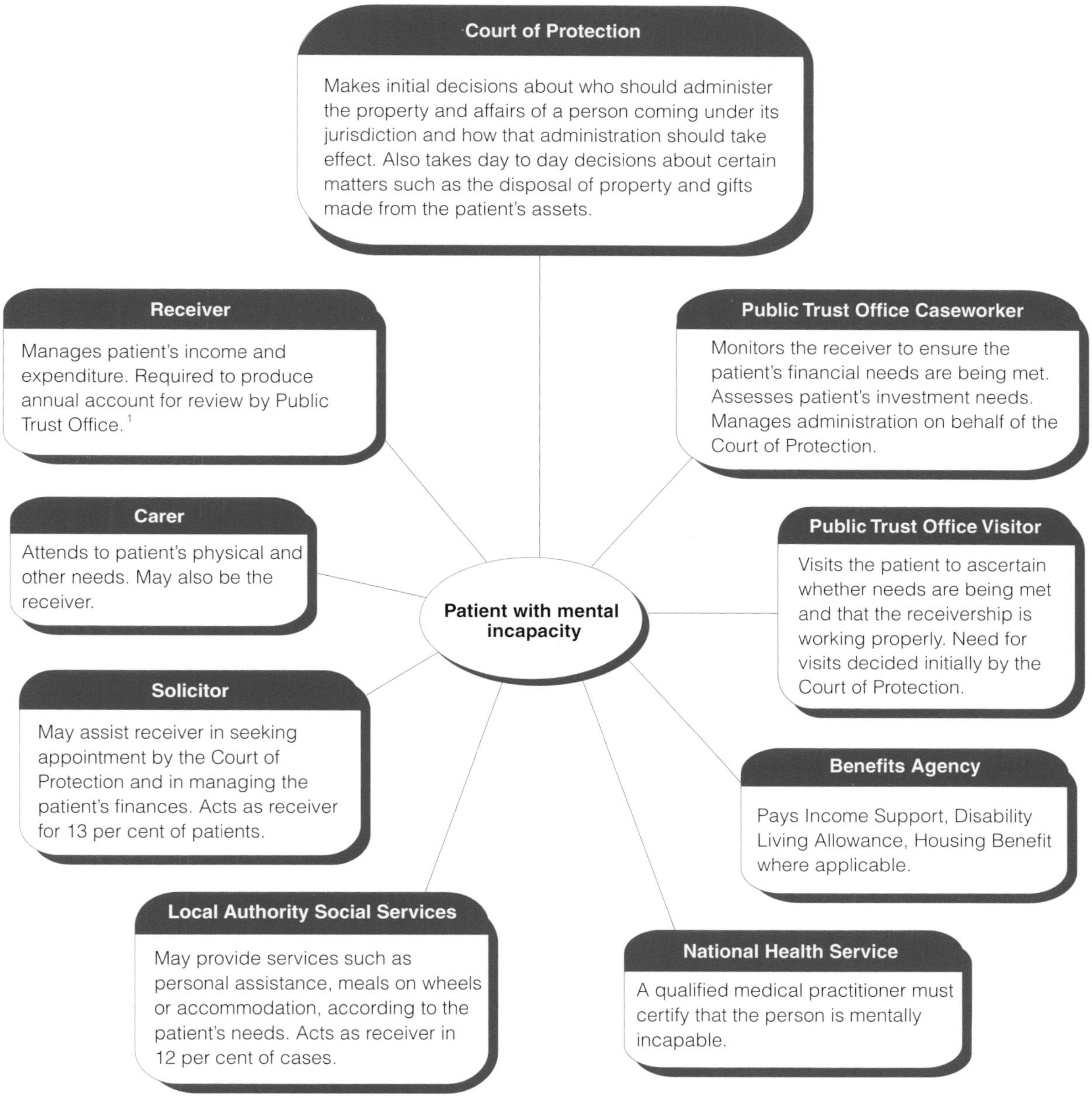

Note 1: In cases where the Public Trustee acts as receiver, the actions of the receiver are undertaken by a Public Trust Office caseworker.

Source: National Audit Office

Key developments since 1994

1.9 The Public Trust Office became an executive agency within the Lord Chancellor's Department in 1994. A Chief Executive (who combines this role with those of the Public Trustee and Accountant General of the Supreme Court) heads the agency and is responsible to the Lord Chancellor for its effective and efficient management. The Lord Chancellor's Department allocates resources to the Public Trust Office, approves its corporate and business plans, including its key performance targets, and determines the level of any performance bonus paid to the Chief Executive.

1.10 The Court of Protection has no jurisdiction over the personal welfare of patients other than in financial, legal or property matters. However, it does have a duty to take personal welfare into account when exercising jurisdiction over the patient's property and affairs. In 1995, the Law Commission reported on the arrangements for all types of decision-making on behalf of mentally incapacitated adults following research and consultation over the previous five years. Its report "Mental Incapacity" (Law Com 231) proposed changes which would have significant implications for the future role and duties of the Public Trust Office, since they envisaged new responsibilities for the Court, including a direct interest in healthcare and personal welfare of people with a mental incapacity. A summary of the relevant Law Commission proposals is at Appendix 3.

1.11 In December 1997, the Government issued a Green Paper "Who Decides?" as part of a consultation process on whether and how the Law Commission's recommendations should be implemented. The Green Paper stated that there was a clear need to reform the law in order to improve and clarify decision-making for those unable to take decisions for themselves, and to provide sufficient protection for mentally incapacitated adults and those who look after them.

Scope and methods of this examination

1.12 The judicial decisions made by the Court of Protection are not for us to examine, but the Court and the Public Trust Office work closely, and in the management and organisation of receivership work the distinction between administrative and judicial functions is not always clear.

1.13 The matters covered in this report are largely the remit of the Mental Health Sector, which employs 370 of the 570 staff of the Public Trust Office (Figure 5). The Public Trust Office's Investment Division provides advisory services to all parts of the Public Trust Office, but only that part of the Division's work which supports the financial affairs of people with mental incapacity is examined in this report. The report also examines financial management and accounting arrangements which apply to the Public Trust Office as a whole.

1.14 The Public Trust Office's remit extends beyond supporting the Court of Protection in its responsibility for the mentally incapacitated. These other responsibilities, which involve about one-third of the staff of the Public Trust Office are not covered in this report. They include, for example, the administration of estates and trusts and minors' awards lodged with courts.

1.15 This report examines the progress by the Public Trust Office since our 1994 report in relation to the financial affairs of people with mental incapacity and considers in particular:

Part 2 - monitoring receivers

Part 3 - visiting patients

Part 4 - managing patients' capital

Part 5 - financial management

Part 6 - customer service.

1.16 We interviewed officials and examined papers at the Public Trust Office, and obtained views of visitors to patients by means of a questionnaire. We sought the views of the Master of the Court of Protection on the issues addressed by our study and also those of a number of national organisations concerned with the care and support of people with mental health problems. Three hundred and ninety-five case files were examined as described in Appendix 4, which sets out the study methodology.

Part 2: Monitoring receivers

2.1   This part of the report examines the Public Trust Office's monitoring of receiverships established to safeguard the interests of the individuals under the jurisdiction of the Court of Protection. It deals first with private receiverships, focusing on progress since 1994 in:

■   ensuring that receivers account for the use of patients' income;

■   reviewing receivers' accounts; and

■   targeting monitoring at those most at risk.

It also considers the Public Trust Office's role where the Public Trustee is appointed receiver and where the Court approves the registration of an Enduring Power of Attorney. The process of appointing a receiver is outlined at Figure 1.

Private receiverships

Ensuring that receivers account for use of patients' income

2.2   The duties of a receiver can be onerous (Figure 7). The receiver is accountable to the Court of Protection for all money received and paid out on behalf of the patient. The Court order setting out the terms of a receivership specifies the basis on which the receiver has to account for their use of the patient's income. Submission of an account is an important part of the receiver's duties, and the Public Trust Office asks referees to comment specifically on a proposed receiver's ability to prepare such an account. To assist receivers, the Public Trust Office provides guidance on what should and should not be included in the account, and the supporting documentation it will need to see.

Responsibilities of receivers

Figure 7

"Duties of a receiver" is one of a number of information leaflets the Public Trust Office provides for the public. It explains that receivers are expected to:

- act at all times in the best interests of the mentally incapacitated person
- safeguard the person's assets
- open a receivership account at a local bank or building society
- claim from the Benefits Agency all social security benefits to which the person is entitled
- take out security and any bond premiums as and when required
- prepare accounts annually or as and when required
- ensure that the person's funds are being used to provide him or her with the best possible quality of life
- ensure that all income is collected and bills are paid on time
- arrange safe keeping of all deeds, documents of title, testamentary documents and other valuable items
- keep any property in a reasonable state of repair and adequately insured
- deal with the person's income tax and other tax matters
- notify the Public Trust Office of any changes in the person's financial situation, for example if the person inherits property or money
- inform the Driver and Vehicle Licensing Authority if the person holds or applies for a driving licence
- advise the Public Trust Office if there is a likelihood of the person getting married, divorced or involved in other legal proceedings
- advise the Public Trust Office if the preparation of a will is being considered
- co-operate with visitors appointed by the Public Trust Office
- obtain the Public Trust Office's permission before dealing with any capital monies
- inform the Public Trust Office of the person's recovery or their death
- pay the Public Trust Office's fees out of the person's monies as and when requested
- inform the Public Trust Office of any change in the person's address
- comply with all Directions and Orders from the Court of Protection

Source : Public Trust Office booklet "Duties of a Receiver"

2.3 An account is normally required annually. The Public Trust Office provides all private receivers with a form of annual account, which usually comprises a simple receipts and payments account showing how the receiver has spent the income received on behalf of the patient, together with any balance left over at the end of the year. The account has to be submitted with supporting documentation such as building society pass books and bank statements. In approximately one-third of cases, where a close relative, a local authority or a solicitor is appointed receiver, the Court of Protection requires less detailed information in the form of an "annual enquiry". In this respect, the Court treats all local authorities alike, although the Law Society and the Association of Directors of Social Services have pointed out that local authorities operate different practices and procedures and have varying levels of involvement as receivers.

2.4 Private receivers are required to submit accounts promptly to enable the Public Trust Office to review them in good time, and to ensure that any points arising from the review can be taken on board by the receiver for the following year. It asks receivers to submit accounts within a month of the anniversary of the receivership. In its 1994 report, the Committee of Public Accounts asked the Public Trust Office to ensure that all annual accounts were submitted promptly. At the time, the Public Trust Office and the Court of Protection were already discussing how this might be achieved.

2.5 Our most recent examination found that almost 40 per cent of receivers had not submitted an account for 1996-97, as required under their terms of appointment. The Public Trust Office told us that it had focused its staff resources on day-to-day casework at the expense of rigorous action to pursue outstanding accounts. It accepted the need for improved management information on the number and proportion of receivers' accounts outstanding.

2.6 Our examination of a sample of accounts also showed that the timeliness of submission by private receivers had deteriorated substantially since our last report which reviewed accounts submission in 1992-93. Only 11 per cent of the accounts we sampled had been submitted on time in 1996-97, against 46 per cent in 1992-93. Almost 20 per cent of accounts were more than six months' late, compared to only 5 per cent at the time of our previous examination in 1994.

2.7 The Public Trust Office's caseworkers are expected to send written reminders to receivers where accounts are three months' overdue. We examined the follow-up action taken on the accounts in our sample which were more than 12 months' overdue and found that in over 40 per cent of cases the caseworker had not sent a written reminder. Whilst the caseworker may in some instances have been in telephone contact with the receiver this was not noted on the file. Examples of overdue accounts are provided in Cases 3 and 4.

Examples of receivers not submitting accounts

Case 3

The son of a 71 year-old patient with senile dementia was appointed her receiver in May 1993. At the time of our examination accounts were outstanding for 1995-96 and 1996-97. The receiver last accounted, for the 1994-95 year, in September 1995.

Case 4

A patient's sister has been acting as receiver for him since July 1988. An account of how she has handled her brother's income and expenditure has been outstanding since July 1996. A premium on the security bond required by the Court of Protection has not been paid. In April 1997, the Public Trust Office released £2,600 to the receiver to fund a holiday for the patient, the receiver and two other relatives.

2.8 The Public Trust Office does not have a procedure in place to check that caseworkers follow up accounts which are more than three months' overdue, and report findings to line managers. It agreed such a procedure with the Master of the Court of Protection in 1995 but did not implement it. The procedure is now being discussed with the new Master, with a view to operating it in the near future. The absence of prescribed follow-up procedures means that the need for remedial action can easily be overlooked. For example, in nine of the cases we examined (9 per cent), receivers had not submitted a single account since they had been appointed; six of these had one or two accounts outstanding; the remainder had three or more accounts overdue. A number of the receivers who had not submitted timely accounts were solicitors whom the Public Trust Office expects to be prompt in submitting accounts. All but one of the receivers subsequently accounted properly for their use of patients' money.

Recommendation 1

The Public Trust Office should put in place procedures to ensure that late accounts are pursued vigorously by caseworkers with periodic mandatory review by line managers, and that it has up to date and accurate management information on the number and proportion of receivers with outstanding accounts and the action being taken.

2.9 Where receivers persistently fail to account there are a number of sanctions available. Caseworkers may initially try to prompt the receiver's compliance by refusing to release capital or complete an action requested by the receiver until accounts have been filed. However, caseworkers need to ensure that the patient's best interests are not prejudiced by their actions. The ultimate sanction is for the Court of Protection to appoint a new receiver. The Master of the Court told us that he is concerned to ensure that individual receivers with particular problems should not be dealt with too harshly. Since 1994, the Court has replaced 3,455 receivers for a variety of reasons.

Recommendation 2

The Public Trust Office, in consultation with the Court of Protection, should consider the need for effective sanctions against receivers who repeatedly fail to submit accounts promptly.

2.10 To cover the risk of receivers misusing patients' funds, the Court of Protection insists in the majority of cases, approximately two-thirds, that they arrange insurance against the misappropriation of patients' funds. The insurance would normally be expected to cover up to 150 per cent of the patient's annual income or of the money likely to pass through the receiver's hands, whichever is greater. The Court considers the particular circumstances of each case and does not normally require spouses or parents to take out insurance, but generally does so where the receiver is not the patient's only close relative, or where the family relationship of the receiver to the patient is not close. The insurance is arranged through the Public Trust Office, usually with a single broker for a relatively small sum, payable from the patient's assets. For example, it costs £71.50 a year to arrange insurance for £25,000 of income.

2.11 In 1997, the Public Trust Office called in only 13 out of the 13,000 insurance policies held by receivers because they had misappropriated patients' funds. However, caseworkers can seek to encourage receivers to submit outstanding accounts by warning them of the financial consequences of the caseworker being obliged to call in an insurance policy. We believe there is insufficient information on the activities of receivers who fail to submit accounts to judge the possible level of undetected abuse.

2.12 In two-thirds of the receiverships we examined where an annual account was outstanding, and the receiver had not accounted for the money they had received, the Court of Protection had not directed that the receiver take out insurance having regard to the circumstances of the case (paragraph 2.10). In our view the absence of both accounts and insurance means the patient's assets may be at particular risk.

2.13 The Public Trust Office reviews the level of insurance during its annual review of the account and adjusts it to reflect fluctuating levels of income. In our sample, we found that where insurance had been taken out, it had been set below the minimum level in 13 per cent of cases. Where the level of insurance is set too low, as in these cases, it may be inadequate to cover any losses.

Recommendation 3

The Public Trust Office should ensure that the levels of insurance bonds of all patients are regularly reviewed and adjusted where necessary so that patients' incomes are adequately protected.

Reviewing receivers' accounts

2.14 The Public Trust Office checks all private receivers' accounts or annual enquiries (paragraph 2.3) to ensure that all money is accounted for and expenditure is properly charged against the patient's estate. We found that where receivers submitted accounts, their quality was high. Less than three per cent of receivers had been required to resubmit their accounts.

2.15 For the review of accounts to be effective, any errors or omissions discovered must be quickly pursued and resolved. At the time of our previous examination of the Public Trust Office in 1994, it had a target to review 70 per cent of accounts within four weeks of receipt from the receiver, and 65 per cent of annual enquiries within two weeks. We found that the Public Trust Office had bettered its target for accounts, with 85 per cent cleared within four weeks. For annual enquiries however, only 60 per cent were being cleared within two weeks. The Committee of Public Accounts expressed concern and said it expected the Public Trust Office to review accounts and enquiries soon after they had been received.

2.16 In response, the Public Trust Office set a target to complete 80 per cent of private receivership account and annual enquiry reviews within four weeks of receipt. We examined performance against the target in 1996-97. Figure 8 shows that around one quarter of the private receivers' accounts in our sample had been reviewed within four weeks of receipt. This compared with the target of 80 per cent and with 85 per cent for accounts submitted in 1992-93, which were considered in our previous report. About one fifth of reviews were conducted more than three months after the accounts had been received.

2.17 The Public Trust Office reported internally that it had reviewed 46 per cent of private receivership accounts within 28 days. Examination of our sample showed that the date of receipt of the receiver's account was not being consistently recorded on the management information system which generated the internal performance figures. Eleven per cent of the sampled cases had been recorded as having met the review target, but in fact took longer than 28 days from receipt of the account to complete the review.

Time taken to review private receivers accounts during 1996-97

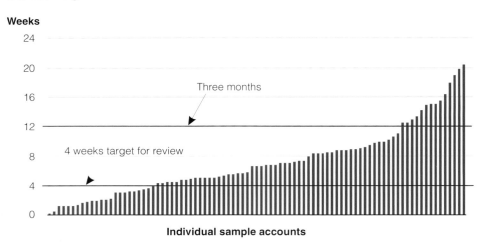

Figure 8

Three quarters of private receivers' accounts in our sample were not reviewed within the four week target.

Source: National Audit Office sample analysis of accounts reviewed during 1996-97

2.18 Our estimate of 25 per cent of accounts reviewed within the deadline is subject to a margin of error of plus or minus 9 per cent to take account of sampling error; this gives a range of 16 to 34 per cent for actual performance against target for all accounts. Figure 9 shows that, even if actual performance were at the higher level of 34 per cent, this would still be well below the target of 80 per cent and represent a substantial deterioration compared with the 85 per cent achieved in 1992-93. The Public Trust Office told us that the deterioration in the proportion of accounts reviewed promptly had resulted from the need to focus staff resources on carrying out casework to ensure that patients' financial affairs were properly protected. When money became available in 1996 and 1997, it had been spent on overtime working to clear the arrears. We noted, however, that the situation had deteriorated further in 1997-98, and that a maximum of 30 per cent of receivers' accounts were reviewed within four weeks.

Recommendation 4

The Public Trust Office should review private receivership accounts promptly so that effective and timely use can be made of the results of the review.

Proportion of private receivers' accounts reviewed within four weeks in 1992-93 and 1996-97

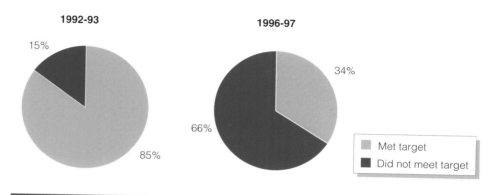

Figure 9

Performance in reviewing private receivers' accounts within four weeks has deteriorated considerably between 1992-93 and 1996-97. Public Trust Office figures for 1997-98 show further deterioration over the 1996-97 figures.

1992-93

15%

85%

1996-97

34%

66%

☐ Met target

■ Did not meet target

2.19 The review of accounts is not undertaken by the caseworker but by a separate branch of the Public Trust Office. It is a basic check to ensure that receivers have accounted for all patients' income received and that payments made in the year were a proper charge against the patients' estate. We concluded from our detailed examination of the review of 30 accounts that the quality of the reviewers' work was good. For example, in all the cases examined the reviewer had correctly recalculated the account where necessary and noted minor mistakes on file. About one-third of the accounts were passed without query. The majority of reviewers' queries arising on the other accounts were administrative, such as the need for staff to update records.

2.20 Up to November 1997, the review concentrated on the accuracy of the account based on the evidence provided to support details of receipts and payments. It did not specifically check that all income due to the patient had been properly claimed and paid into their account. The Public Trust Office has now widened the scope of the review to check, for example, whether the patient is receiving all the social security benefits to which they are entitled.

2.21 The review of annual accounts triggers a wider review of each patient's case. However, since 40 per cent of receivers had not submitted an account in 1996-97, and only 11 per cent submitted their accounts on time, many cases could not be promptly reviewed. We believe that the absence of an account may in itself signal that the patient's case needs urgent consideration.

2.22 The wider review focuses on whether receivers are discharging their responsibilities to the patient and to the Court of Protection. In 1994, we found that the Public Trust Office had little information to enable it to undertake this review; for example relatively few patients were visited each year, and visits were not in any case linked to the review cycle for accounts. To provide this information, we recommended that receivers be required to submit an annual statement on the patient's needs over the coming year and a scheme of maintenance. The Public Trust Office subsequently required receivers to submit such a statement along with the annual account of their stewardship of patients' finances. However, this information is not available in those cases where receivers do not submit accounts.

Using risk assessment

2.23 In early 1994, the Public Trust Office commissioned management consultants to review its work processes and to identify and evaluate opportunities for improvement. The consultants recommended the use of risk assessment to improve the ability to respond to the rising workload. The recommended approach (Figure 10) required managers and caseworkers to identify characteristics of a receivership to enable them to determine the best balance between the receiver's authority to act for the patient and the associated risk for the patient. As part of the assessment, the Public Trust Office would look at how closely it needed to monitor each receivership. Receivers assessed as low risk would be given authority to take decisions which normally required the approval of the Public Trust Office or the Court of Protection. In addition, the caseworker would have authority to release the patient's capital to the receiver when income generated was insufficient to meet the patient's needs. Receivers assessed as high risk would be subject to more detailed scrutiny. Caseworker time would thus be concentrated on those receiverships identified as high risk.

Method for assessing risk and determining the level of authority to be granted to the receiver

Figure 10

Receiver and patient characteristics should be profile.

Characteristics of the receiver include his/her relationship with the patient; the type of applicant (individual, professional, local authority etc.); age of receiver; experience in managing financial matters; responsibility or authority requested; whether the receiver's application is contested.

Characteristics of the patient include age; life expectancy; care arrangements; income and capital at the patient's disposal.

The Public Trust Office should obtain a comprehensive assessment of expenditure, not just of regular payments made on behalf of the patient, but of the total expenditure likely to be incurred annually and over the patient's lifetime.

The receiver's willingness and ability to act under a wider authority should be assessed under a financial threshold determined by the comprehensive assessment of expenditure.

Source: 1994 consultants' report on Public Trust Office's business processes

2.24 The Public Trust Office piloted limited aspects of the approach in 1995 and has since adopted them in the assessment of new private receiverships, and of existing private receiverships at the time of the review of the annual account. As a result:

■ Receivers' characteristics are now assessed: for example solicitors, accountants, local authorities, parents and spouses are generally classified as low risk; other receivers are generally classified as medium risk; contested receiverships are considered high risk. However, the competence of the receiver to administer the financial affairs of the patient is not assessed as this is a matter for the Court of Protection when appointing a receiver.

■ The characteristics of the patient are now taken into account in determining their financial needs.

2.25 The risk assessment determines the extent to which capital will be released for the care of patients and the type of account to be submitted by receivers (whether full or the simplified annual enquiry). New receivers are assessed at the start of the case and existing receivers are assessed annually, on producing their accounts. However, those receivers who fail to account may have never been risk assessed, though caseworkers are instructed to consider restricting access to capital for receivers whose accounts are six months late. The Public Trust Office is continuing to implement the consultants' 1994 recommendations on risk assessment and is considering a more fundamental streamlining of its monitoring process.

Recommendation 5	The Public Trust Office should develop risk assessment of private receiverships to include factors such as the receiver's track record in meeting their responsibilities as a receiver, with a view to focusing on those receivers where patients' funds appear to be most at risk.

Recommendation 6	The Public Trust Office should consider, with the Court of Protection, greater delegation of authority to low risk receivers.

Public Trustee receiverships

2.26 In approximately 11 per cent of cases, the Court of Protection appoints the Public Trustee as receiver in response to a direct application or because no one else is willing and able to act as receiver. A caseworker from the Public Trust Office undertakes the day-to-day administration of the receivership and carries out many of the receiver's responsibilities detailed in Figure 7. The caseworker has to maintain regular contact with the mentally incapacitated person, relatives, social workers and professional advisers. While the Public Trustee's responsibilities as receiver relate solely to the patient's financial affairs, in practice caseworkers cannot ignore welfare issues, especially where the patient has no relatives and looks to the caseworker for advice in resolving problems that may not be of a financial nature.

2.27 On the anniversary of the receivership, a computer automatically generates annual accounts providing a full listing of all transactions undertaken on the patient's behalf. To ensure that the work of the Public Trustee as receiver is discharged properly and in the best interests of the patient, the production and subsequent review of the accounts are carried out by separate sections of the Public Trust Office, which are independent of the caseworker. The frequency of review is determined using a risk assessment based on the complexity of the receivership, including the type of social security benefits claimed. Higher risk receiverships are reviewed every year and lower risk receiverships every two years. The caseworker acting as receiver is not told the results of the risk analysis, and is therefore generally unaware of the degree of scrutiny that will be applied to each case.

2.28 At the time of our previous examination in 1994, we found a backlog of some 868 Public Trustee receivership accounts awaiting review, some of which had been available more than eighteen months earlier. The Committee of Public Accounts considered it unsatisfactory that such a large backlog of accounts had been allowed to build up. By temporarily dedicating resources to the task, the Public Trust Office cleared the backlog by September 1994.

2.29 In 1993, the Public Trust Office had a target of reviewing 50 per cent of Public Trustee receivership accounts within eight weeks. Since then it has set a more demanding target of reviewing 80 per cent of accounts within eight weeks. The Public Trust Office's local records show a significant improvement in performance since 1992-93 with, for example, 89 per cent of accounts being reviewed within eight weeks in 1996-97 (Figure 11). However, in our sample of 1996-97 cases we found that only one third of accounts had been reviewed within eight weeks. The reason for these different findings is that the Public Trust Office has recorded some accounts which have taken up to 13 weeks to be reviewed as having met the eight week target. Our findings, based on actual timescales of cases in the sample, suggest that there has actually been a deterioration in the time taken to review accounts since 1992-93 (Figure 11).

Proportion of Public Trustee receivership accounts reviewed within eight weeks in 1992-93 and 1996-97

Figure 11

Public Trust Office data show an improved performance since 1992-93. However our estimate of performance based on a sample of 50 cases suggests that performance has deteriorated and that the Public Trust Office has misinterpreted the target and thus overstated performance.

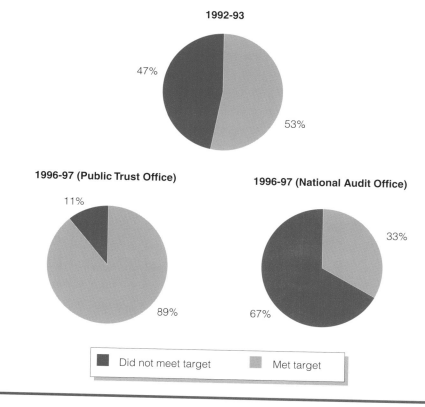

1992-93

47%

53%

1996-97 (Public Trust Office)

11%

89%

1996-97 (National Audit Office)

33%

67%

Did not meet target   Met target

Source: National Audit Office examination of 50 case files

Recommendation 7	The Public Trust Office should review Public Trustee receivership accounts promptly so that effective and timely use can be made of the results of the review.

2.30 The account and case reviews conducted for Public Trustee cases are more thorough and wide ranging than for private receivers. Specific questions require detailed responses from the reviewer and from the caseworker acting as receiver. For example, the review covers the completeness and accuracy of benefit claims, the appropriateness of investment policy and returns, and the adequacy of work done by the caseworker as a receiver. All points raised by the reviewer are referred to the caseworker who has a fixed timescale within which to reply with a satisfactory explanation for the action taken or a note that remedial action will be taken. The results of reviews are held on a computer database which is used to analyse errors and trends, and to help senior management in identifying where improvements in procedures might be made.

Enduring Powers of Attorney

2.31 An ordinary Power of Attorney is not valid after the onset of mental incapacity in the person who has made it, (the donor). However, the donor can execute an Enduring Power of Attorney (EPA) to appoint a person of their choice to administer their affairs and this power is valid after the onset of mental incapacity. It must be drawn up whilst the individual is mentally capable and able to select the person to whom the power is given. The attorney must immediately register the power with the Public Trust Office if the donor is, or if they think the donor is, becoming mentally incapable. The power can specify particular areas to be managed, such as property or business transactions.

2.32 EPAs came about as a result of the Law Commission's consideration of two conflicting needs: to provide a simple, effective and inexpensive method of allowing ordinary Powers of Attorney to continue on incapacity; and to protect the donor's interests against exploitation. By making an EPA, the donor chooses the person they trust to look after their affairs in the event that they become mentally incapable. They can, as a result, also avoid the costs of a full receivership. A single registration fee of £50 is payable to the Public Trust Office for an EPA. Receivership fees are considerably higher than this because they need to cover the Public Trust Office's monitoring and continuing administrative costs.

2.33 There were over 40,000 EPAs registered with the Public Trust Office at 31 March 1998. Not all EPAs submitted for registration are valid, mainly due to legal flaws in them. In 1997-98 there were around 9,900 applications and 8,100 registrations. In recent years, the Public Trust Office has encouraged the use of EPAs and has set up a separate section to process registration. The Law Society told us that it welcomed these developments which had helped to concentrate expertise and improve registration times.

2.34 Under the Enduring Power of Attorney Act 1985, the Court of Protection may require the attorney appointed under the terms of an EPA to account to it for their dealings with the donor's finances. The Public Trust Office informs people enquiring about EPAs that it is always advisable to keep accounts when dealing with someone else's money. To date, the Court has required attorneys to produce accounts in only a handful of cases, usually following a request or expression of concern from a third party (Cases 5 and 6). Even then, the attorney does not always provide accounts and by resigning the attorneyship is removed from the jurisdiction of the Court and its power to require accounts.

Abuses of Enduring Powers of Attorney

Case 5

The donor's two grandsons were jointly granted an Enduring Power of Attorney. The Public Trust Office subsequently received a letter from the attorney's solicitor suggesting that proceeds from the sale of the donor's house had been invested in the attorney's business. The Public Trust Office requested details of the donor's assets, income and expenditure, but the attorneys disappeared. Investigation of the donor's bank account revealed that £35,500, including the net proceeds of the sale of the donor's house, had been withdrawn and no benefit received by the donor.

Case 6

An Enduring Power of Attorney was granted to the donor's friend without any objections being received. One month later the donor's doctor contacted the Public Trust Office questioning the donor's mental capability at the time of signing the power. The attorney immediately disclaimed the power but investigation of the donor's assets to enable a receiver to be appointed revealed a missing property. The police investigated and found that the attorney had sold the property for £29,000 but had given only £1,500 to the donor. The attorney was convicted of fraud, given a two year suspended sentence and fined £500.

2.35 although the legislation does provide for checks on accounts, the Court of Protection does not usually require the Public Trust Office to make checks, and the Public Trust Office has no statutory duty to do so. The Master of the Court pointed out that donors have deliberately entrusted their financial affairs into the hands of the attorney, in the knowledge that their activities are unlikely to be monitored. Because the Court does not require routine monitoring, it is not possible to attempt to estimate the extent of abuse of EPAs but Cases 5 and 6 show that it does occur.

2.36 The Law Commission has recommended that the EPA be replaced by a Continuing Power of Attorney. This would also continue beyond the onset of mental incapacity but would address health care and personal welfare decisions as well as financial affairs (Appendix 3). The proposals for Continuing Powers of Attorney do not include extending the need for attorneys to provide accounts.

Recommendation 8

The Lord Chancellor's Department and the Court of Protection should consider what safeguards should accompany the registration system for Enduring Powers of Attorney and the fees that would be necessary to fund such work.

Part 3: Visiting patients

3.1 The Court of Protection has no jurisdiction over the person or personal welfare of patients other than in financial, legal or property matters. However, it does have a duty to take personal welfare matters into account when exercising its jurisdiction over a patient's property and affairs. Visits to patients provide the Public Trust Office with knowledge of their circumstances and well-being, and can bring immediate benefits to them by identifying ways in which their quality of life can be improved. For private receivership cases, visits are an opportunity to provide direct feedback to the Public Trust Office on how well a receivership is operating, and can alert it to action required to ensure that the needs of patients are properly addressed (Case 7). Where the Public Trustee acts as receiver, visitors should act as the eyes and ears of the Public Trust Office, gathering information essential to the patient's welfare and the effective running of their estate. Visitors do not have any responsibility to review patients' financial affairs.

Illustrating the value of visits to patients

Case 7

Mrs C is a 97 year-old woman with Alzheimer's disease living in a private nursing home. She has no close relatives and a solicitor was appointed as her receiver in 1996. A visitor employed by the Public Trust Office visited her for the first time in January 1997. The visitor considered the patient urgently needed new clothing. On receiving the report from the visitor, the patient's caseworker wrote to the receiver to ask him to arrange for new clothing. Clothing was purchased and a further visit to check on progress was also arranged.

3.2 In 1994, the Committee of Public Accounts considered that the number of private receivership visits being conducted was unacceptably low and recommended the Public Trust Office consider carefully whether the visiting arrangements then in place were achieving the right balance between cost and protection of patients. This part of the report examines:

■ progress since 1994 in improving visiting arrangements;

■ the frequency and geographic distribution of visits; and

■ whether the most is made of visits to patients.

Visiting arrangements

3.3   At the time of our 1994 examination, self-employed visitors commissioned by the Public Trust Office visited Public Trustee patients. Staff of the welfare branch of the Lord Chancellor's Department made visits to private receivers' patients. They were not specifically trained for the work and accorded it low priority.

3.4   The Public Trust Office and the Lord Chancellor's Department subsequently accepted that patients would be best served by a dedicated visiting service under the Public Trust Office's control. Responsibility for private receivership visits was transferred from the Lord Chancellor's Department to the Public Trust Office from April 1996, together with annual funding of £170,000, comprising £40,000 for support staff and overheads and £130,000 for visits. The Public Trust Office decided to use self-employed visitors who are paid £65 per visit, permitting a maximum of 2,000 visits per year at a full cost of £85 per visit. In 1995-96, the last full year of visits by staff of the Lord Chancellor's Department, the cost per visit had been £225. The Public Trust Office has, therefore, made efficiency savings of £140 per visit as a result of these changed arrangements which, in a full year, should enable more than twice as many people to be visited compared with 1995-96 under the previous arrangements. Private receivership patients do not pay directly for visits, but Public Trustee patients pay from £7 to £88 per visit according to their income.

3.5   The appointment of new visitors was not publicly advertised. In July 1996 six people were appointed to undertake visits from a list of 18 candidates who had expressed an interest. Four of the six were former staff of the Public Trust Office or the Lord Chancellor's Department; one had been a receiver for a relative; and one was an approved social worker under the 1983 Mental Health Act. The selection procedures were designed to ensure that the best of the 18 candidates were offered the work. However, public advertising might have attracted more qualified mental health workers or people with direct experience of working with the mentally incapacitated.

Recommendation 9   The Public Trust Office should publicly advertise visitor work, so that applicants with wider experience of dealing with people with mental incapacity are able to apply.

Frequency and distribution of visits

Public Trustee receivership patients

3.6 For patients for whom the Public Trustee is the receiver visits are especially important, because otherwise the Public Trust Office would have to rely solely on the limited information the patient or carer could provide by correspondence or telephone. The visit gives the caseworker, acting on behalf of the Public Trustee, information on the living conditions and needs of the patient.

3.7 The Public Trust Office needs to carry out visits with reasonable frequency to help it consider changes in a patient's circumstances and to respond promptly and effectively to any problems. Its aim therefore is to ensure that all Public Trustee patients are visited at least once a year. For a small proportion of patients, such as those who live abroad or who refuse a visit, a visit may not be made. Figure 12 shows that 86 per cent of patients were visited within 12 months in 1992-93, but only two-thirds received visits within 12 months in 1996-97. The number of patients visited within 18 months showed a smaller reduction from 97 to 92 per cent respectively. The Public Trust Office told us that the number of visits carried out in 1996-97 was affected by the long-term sickness absence of one of the visitors.

Timing of the most recent visit to Public Trustee patients

Figure 12

Fewer patients subject to Public Trustee receiverships are being visited within twelve months than in 1992-93.

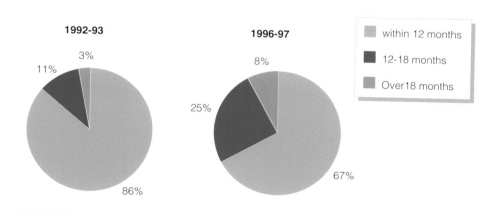

1992-93

3%
11%
86%

1996-97

8%
25%
67%

within 12 months
12-18 months
Over18 months

Source: 1994 National Audit Office report and examination of visits made during 1996-97

Recommendation 10

The Public Trust Office should improve its monitoring of visits to Public Trustee receivership patients and ensure that visits are made to all patients each year unless, exceptionally, the patient's circumstances do not warrant a visit.

Private receivership patients

3.8 The Court of Protection determines which private receivership patients should receive an initial visit. According to the Court's 1988 direction, patients need not be visited:

- where the patient is resident in a National Health Service hospital (10 per cent);

- where a local authority acts as receiver (12 per cent); and

- where the patient lives in a residential or nursing home and receives regular visits by the receiver, relatives, friends or neighbours (just under two-thirds of patients reside in homes; the number receiving regular visits is not easily quantifiable, but the Public Trust Office considers that the majority are visited).

The Court of Protection's direction meant that a minimum of 22 per cent of private receivership patients would never receive a visit from visitors appointed by the Public Trust Office. The Public Trust Office estimated that 75 to 80 per cent of patients are excluded by the above criteria but does not have full information on patients to confirm this estimate. Age Concern told us that local authorities often do not have regular programmes for visiting patients in their role as receivers. They were concerned that this could mean that some patients might not receive a visit from either the local authority or the Public Trust Office.

3.9 During our examination, we discussed with the Public Trust Office whether the 1988 direction was still appropriate. On the advice of the Public Trust Office, the Court of Protection has revised the criteria and the changes have been implemented. These include, for example, a requirement to make at least one visit to those patients whose receivers are local authorities and to minors. The Public Trust Office told us that within both the previous and the new criteria there is no discretion for it specifically to target visits towards, for example, patients whose receivers have failed to submit accounts.

3.10 Patients not excluded by the Court of Protection's 1988 direction were placed on a visitors' list. Patients may require visits on an annual, biennial, triennial or one-off basis. The Public Trust Office has conflicting details of the number of patients on the list, as its main computer record is believed to be inaccurate, but estimated the total at between 3,300 and 3,700. As a result there appears to be some uncertainty over the level of outstanding visits at any one time. A manual record is used to manage the visiting programme.

Recommendation 11

The Public Trust Office should improve its management information on patients to be visited, the required frequency of visits, and actual visits made in order to provide assurance to management that visit requirements for individual patients are being met.

3.11 Figure 13 shows the number of visits made to private receivership patients between 1992-93 and 1997-98. In both 1996-97 and 1997-98, the first two full years of the new arrangements (paragraph 3.4), almost 1,700 visits were made. This was just over 10 per cent more than in 1992-93 when the Committee of Public Accounts considered the level of visits (1,500) to be unacceptably low for a maximum visitable population of 14,000 patients. The 1992-93 level was however higher than usual because the Public Trust Office committed extra resources to tackling a developing backlog. A backlog of over 1,100 visits to patients with private receivers at April 1993 was reduced to 214 by April 1997. The 1,680 visits carried out in 1997-98 were double the level of around 800 completed both in 1994-95 and 1995-96. The Public Trust Office believes that it visits all the patients it is required to visit each year.

Number of visits made to private receivership patients, 1992-93 to 1997-98

Figure 13

Almost 1700 visits were made in 1996-97 and 1997-98 following the introduction of the new visiting arrangements. In 1997-98, the number of visits was just over ten per cent above the 1992-93 level - 1,500 - a figure the Committee of Public Accounts had considered unacceptably low.

Number of Visits

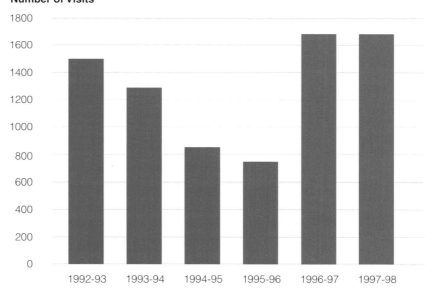

Source: 1994 National Audit Office report and examination of Public Trust Office records of visits made

Note: 1992-93 and 1993-94 totals include a number of visits completed as part of a special exercise using ex-Public Trust Office staff as general visitors

3.12 The Court of Protection's policy is that all patients eligible for a visit should receive an early visit, and that the visitor should then recommend whether the patient requires further visits or not. In 1996-97 visitors recommended further visits in almost three-quarters of cases, although the recommendation was often for visits only every two or three years.

3.13 In 1994, we suggested that the Court of Protection might consider setting out the criteria for selecting patients for repeat visits and for prioritising urgent cases. When it took over responsibility for appointing visitors, the Public Trust Office drew up guidance on the matter. Visitors' recommendations are based on this guidance with the final decision resting with the patient's caseworker.

3.14 When patients are removed from the visitor's list, it is still possible for caseworkers, after referral to a senior officer, to recommend that the patient be visited again at some later date. However, there are no criteria to guide such decisions. Since November 1997, there has been a requirement for the caseworker to review the need for repeat visits as part of the review of the receiver's annual account. Several visitors' reports we examined recommended no further visit be conducted so long as there were no changes in the patient's family circumstances, but caseworkers are not required to draw attention to such changes.

Recommendation 12

The Public Trust Office should assess whether, for patients removed from the visit list, adequate trigger points exist to keep the position under review so that they are returned promptly to the list where changes in personal circumstances are such that visits should be resumed.

Recommendation 13

The Public Trust Office should consider whether current arrangements for visiting are the most appropriate, or whether alternative arrangements, perhaps involving local organisations, with appropriate quality controls, or the appointment of additional visitors would enable more local delivery of visits.

3.15 The Public Trust Office manually records data on the characteristics of the patients visited, the recommendations made by visitors, and the action taken following visits. However this is not routinely analysed to provide management information on the visits programme. This, in turn, prevents any evaluation of whether the visits programme is well targeted or an effective use of limited visitor resources, within the existing visiting criteria. We compared the distribution of visits per 1,000 visitable patients between visitors' areas. There was a consistent level in four regions, but the Northern region had significantly more and the London region fewer visits per 1,000 patients than the other four regions (Figure 14). This may reflect differences in the characteristics of patients in different regions, but could also arise from different visiting policies, for example with respect to repeat visits. At present the Public Trust Office does not collect sufficient, relevant management information to enable it to determine whether the limited resources available for visiting patients are being used to best effect.

Visits to private receivership patients per 1000 visitable patients in each visiting region

Figure 14

There are wide differences in the number of visits per 1000 patients in the visiting regions, particularly between London and the North.

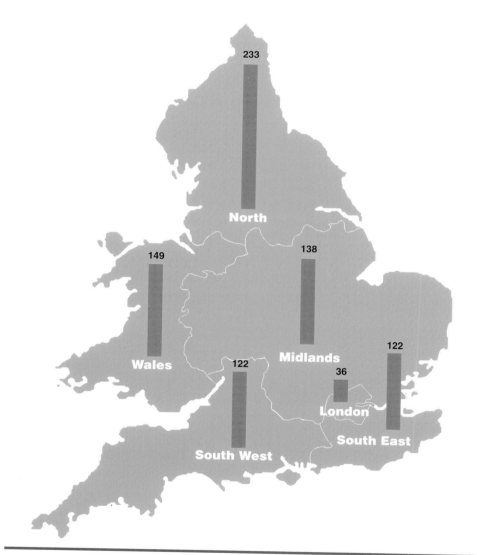

Source: National Audit Office analysis of Public Trust Office records of visits

Recommendation 14	The Public Trust Office should monitor whether visitors are applying the guidance on repeat visits consistently.

Recommendation 15	The Public Trust Office should improve and computerise its management information on visits to patients to ensure that visits are concentrated on patients with the greatest need and investigate the reasons for the wide differences in the visiting rates across regions.

Making the most of visits to patients

3.16 Bringing visitors directly under the control of the Court of Protection and the Public Trust Office provided an opportunity to integrate their work more closely with that of caseworkers. We examined 50 visitors' reports and obtained views from all current visitors and from Public Trust Office staff on how arrangements were operating in practice.

3.17 In one quarter of the 50 reports examined, the visitor had concluded that the receivership was operating satisfactorily and recommended no further action. In the remaining cases, the visitor considered a further visit would be of use to the Court of Protection in monitoring the receivership. One fifth of the 50 reports included specific recommendations for the caseworker to consider action to improve the patient's quality of life, ranging from replacing clothing to ensuring that the receiver took steps to improve the patient's accommodation. The standard of the visit reports was generally high and they provided the Public Trust Office with a clear appreciation of how receiverships were working. The Master of the Court of Protection told us that he valued the work of the visitors highly.

3.18 For visits to make the most effective contribution to case management, there needs to be a dialogue between visitors and caseworkers, timely and useful visit reports, and effective action by the caseworker on any recommendations. All the visitors we spoke to praised the support they receive from their main point of contact, the Public Trust Office's visitors' secretariat. But they believed that the briefing they received from caseworkers could be improved, especially regarding the patient's financial circumstances. On repeat visits, the visitors felt they were often inadequately briefed by the Public Trust Office's staff on changes in the patient's circumstances. In some cases basic details about patients were wrong, occasionally even leading to an abortive visit.

3.19 We found that visitors were concerned that some caseworkers did not act on their recommendations or notify them that no action had been taken on recommendations. They believed such behaviour presented both the Court of Protection and the visitor in an uncaring light on subsequent visits. Visitors also felt that caseworkers should clearly document action taken on the recommendations in visit reports. The Public Trust Office told us visitors' recommendations were not lightly rejected but considered that the caseworker often had more information available on which to make a balanced judgement.

Recommendation 16

The Public Trust Office should ensure that visitors have up-to-date and adequate briefing on patients' circumstances to ensure patients receive maximum benefit from visits.

Part 4: Managing patients' capital

4.1 About half the people who come under the jurisdiction of the Court of Protection have some capital available to invest (Cases 8 and 9). Their estates vary in size and complexity. Most are of £50,000 or less but some are worth more than £1 million. Whereas the management of a patient's income and expenditure is supervised by their receiver, access to their capital is controlled by the Public Trust Office which also supervises or directly manages its investment. In 1997-98, the Public Trust Office supervised the investment of over £1.45 billion of patients' capital (Figure 15).

Examples of patients with funds invested by the Public Trust Office

Case 8

Mrs D suffered serious head injuries and gradually suffered memory loss, loss of concentration and depression. She became vulnerable to exploitation and her daughter was appointed receiver. Her savings of £18,000 were invested in a high interest bearing account available to the Public Trust Office, and the interest contributes to her living expenses.

Case 9

Mr E became severely mentally and physically handicapped following a road traffic accident. He was awarded damages of approximately £300,000. The Court of Protection appointed his father as receiver to manage his income and expenditure; the Public Trust Office took responsibility for managing his capital. With the approval of the receiver, the Public Trust Office invested some of the funds in an interest-bearing deposit account and in following a long term strategy the rest was invested in a segregated portfolio containing a spread of ordinary shares as well as unit trust and investment trusts.

4.2 In 1994, the Committee of Public Accounts recommended that the Public Trust Office should ensure that patients' investment requirements were regularly reviewed, updated and subject to annual performance assessment. This part of the report considers whether the Public Trust Office has successfully done so. In particular it examines:

■ whether the investment needs of patients are adequately assessed;

■ how investment decisions are managed;

■ how the performance of patients' investments is measured;

■ how investments have performed recently; and

■ whether the Public Trust Office has taken steps to review and improve investment performance.

Assessing the investment needs of patients

4.3 When a receiver is appointed, the Court of Protection makes a direction as to the management of the patient's assets and in most cases sets the initial investment requirement for patients. Where necessary, physical assets are liquidated in the most tax efficient way possible. The Public Trust Office, when reviewing a patient's investment requirement, will consider a number of factors: the total value of the resources; the patient's life expectancy; the amount and timing of the return required; at what point capital or additional income may be needed; and the acceptable level of risk. A key judgement concerns the level of income the fund's investment strategy must seek to provide for the patient, and how much the strategy can be geared towards capital growth.

4.4 Patients' circumstances may change over time and the patient's caseworker is therefore expected to keep the investment requirement under review. It should, as a minimum, be reviewed during the annual case review. In most of the cases we examined the caseworker had done this. However, the annual review of private receivership cases is only performed when receivers' accounts are submitted. It had not been possible, therefore, for the caseworker to undertake such a review in the 40 per cent of cases for which no accounts had been submitted in 1996-97.

4.5 Casework reviewers are not expected to have formal training in investment management and monitoring, since such knowledge is not considered essential to enable them to carry out their responsibility for ensuring that funds are available to meet the patient's current needs. The caseworker can, where necessary, refer a case to the Public Trust Office's Investment Division for advice. The Public Trust Office told us that in its experience it is sufficient for caseworkers to consider the need for a review of the investment requirement when they receive information on a material change in the patient's circumstances. A more detailed review of patients' investment needs is carried out where the Public Trustee is the receiver. Here the caseworker has to comment on the continued appropriateness of the investment requirement and the extent to which the current investment policy meets the patient's needs. We found that this review was being carried out thoroughly by caseworkers.

Managing investments

Cash

4.6 The Public Trustee as Accountant General of the Supreme Court is authorised to provide for the transfer of patients' money to and from an account managed by the National Debt Commissioners. Just under half of patients' capital is invested in this account. Such money is referred to as being in "Special Account" (Figure 15). Interest is paid to the patient at a rate specified by the Lord Chancellor with the consent of the Treasury. This interest bearing facility is generally used where the patient's assets are available for investment for less than five years and for the cash element of longer-term investment funds.

Patients' capital managed and invested by the Public Trust Office

Figure 15

Just under half of patients' assets are invested in a short-term deposit account.

Type of Investment	Total sum invested 1997-98 £ million	Proportion of all invested funds (per cent)
Cash on short-term deposit	712	49.3
Securities	734	50.7
Total	**1,446**	**100**

Source: Public Trust Office

Investment portfolios

4.7 Where a patient's assets exceed £150,000 and a long-term investment strategy is desirable, the Public Trust Office arranges for the assets to be invested in a segregated portfolio containing a spread of ordinary shares as well as unit trusts and investment trusts. Advice on the overall investment strategy is provided by the Honorary Investment Advisory Committee, an independent committee of financial experts appointed by the Lord Chancellor. This Committee meets five times a year to review the general market and performance of investments, to give advice, and to make recommendations.

4.8 The portfolios of a minority of private receivership patients, 16 per cent at March 1997, are handled by their own private brokers. This usually occurs where the patient has a long-running business relationship with a broker prior to the appointment of a receiver, and the Court of Protection has authorised the arrangement to continue, subject to review of the broker's investment performance by the Public Trust Office.

4.9 At the time of our examination, the portfolios of the remaining private receivership patients were managed by the Public Trust Office's two "panel" brokers, James Capel Investment Management and Capel-Cure Sharp. The panel brokers were re-appointed by the Public Trust Office in December 1994 for a four-year period following a competitive tender. A former member of the Honorary Investment Advisory Committee chaired the panel which evaluated the tenders, and the competition enabled the Public Trust Office to obtain a competitive scale of commission rates.

4.10 The brokers charge their commission against transactions carried out on behalf of patients. In return, patients receive an investment review, advisory and execution service; an annual capital gains tax review; and a discounted personal equity plan purchase facility. The Public Trust Office told us that these services would normally incur a management fee of one per cent of total assets plus value added tax. It therefore believes that the arrangements with the panel brokers provide good value for money for patients. The patients are generally allocated one of the two panel brokers alphabetically, A-K and L-Z, who are responsible for carrying out at least six-monthly reviews and, in the light of patients' investment requirements, making specific recommendations to receivers. All share dealings require the prior permission of the receiver, and the panel broker then carries out the necessary transactions.

4.11 Where the Public Trustee is the receiver, staff in the Public Trust Office's Investment Division take investment decisions on behalf of the 900 patients with significant assets. The resulting transactions are executed by the panel brokers according to the alphabetical split noted above.

Targets for investment performance

Cash

4.12 The Public Trust Office monitors the rates for cash deposits available to it from the account managed by the National Debt Commissioners (paragraph 4.6) against the rates available for cash deposited on similar terms at building societies and banks. Currently it pays a rate of interest for patients on these funds of eight per cent gross.

Investment portfolios

4.13 The Public Trust Office requires all patients' brokers to provide information on the performance of the portfolios under their management. Each portfolio is valued on the anniversary of the receivership being set up, and performance compared against general market trends. The Public Trust Office follows the capital-only performance standard published by the Association of Private Client Investment Managers and Stockbrokers. The Public Trust Office's targets for the performance of funds are explained in Figure 16 the annual performance target was supplemented by a three-year target in 1996-97, and both measure capital growth, but not income earned on investments.

Measurement of the Public Trust Office's target on investment performance

Figure 16

The Public Trust Office has two targets which measure the one and three-year capital growth of patients' portfolios against a weighted market index.

Target since 1994-95: one year performance

The target is based on a comparison of performance with a weighted market index derived from the Financial Times Stock Exchange 100 and Government Securities' indices. The index is weighted according to the balance of equity and fixed interest securities held in the individual patient's portfolio.

The Public Trust Office measures the annual growth of the portfolio and compares it with the weighted market index. The target is that for at least 85 per cent of portfolios, growth should be at least 95 per cent of the weighted market index.

Target since 1996-97: performance over three years

Measuring year-on-year performance may be inappropriate for many portfolios where the investment strategy is to obtain long-term growth. For this reason, the Public Trust Office established a new performance target in 1996-97 which aims to measure portfolios' performance over a period of three years. The target is that for at least 80 per cent of portfolios, growth should be at least 95 per cent of the weighted market index.

Source: Public Trust Office

The Public Trust Office regards this as more indicative of a portfolio's performance which was predicated on a minimum five-year investment life.

4.14 About 30 per cent of portfolios are excluded from the calculation of performance against the targets each year, usually where the patient's money has not yet been fully invested. Portfolios are also excluded where large sums have been taken out of the portfolio during the year, where a receiver has obstructed transactions (Case 10), or where the broker has inherited a poorly structured portfolio which needs to be sorted out before performance can be measured fairly. The Public Trust Office has recently codified the criteria for excluding portfolios, to reduce the risk of decisions to exclude being made on an inconsistent basis. We suggested that the Public Trust Office should supplement the performance information provided to the Honorary Investment Advisory Committee with information on the numbers of excluded portfolios, along with the reasons for exclusion. In October 1998, the Committee and the Court approved the Public Trust Office's approach to excluding portfolios, including the criteria for exclusion, and the arrangements for logging excluded cases and the reasons for their exclusion.

A receiver obstructing investment transactions

Case 10

The sister of a patient was appointed his receiver. In 1996, the panel broker sought details of the patient's original share purchase as it wished to utilise capital gains tax allowances. The receiver did not respond to that or a further nine separate letters or investment proposals in the period to October 1997. The Public Trust Office noted in January 1998 that the receiver's lack of contact was seriously hindering the management of the portfolio. As the receiver's approval was needed before executing transactions, the lack of any response meant that the patient has been unable to use his capital gains tax allowances in 1996-97 and 1997-98 and other desirable improvements to his portfolio have been obstructed.

4.15 Both the one and three-year investment targets focus on the capital growth of patients' portfolios, not income earned on investments. These are overall targets for the Public Trust Office and do not apply to individual portfolios, which may require a focus on income rather than capital growth. The investment strategy of some 40 per cent of portfolios stipulates high income as well as capital growth, while most of the rest of the portfolios will require some lower level of income as well as capital growth. Since January 1997, alternative published benchmarks have been available through the Association of Private Client Investment Managers and Stockbrokers. These provide capital-only performance indicators for three types of portfolio – growth, income and a balance of income and growth. In the light of this development, the Public Trust Office has set up a working party to consider the methodology of the performance calculation it requires brokers to follow.

4.16 The Public Trust Office announced as its investment target for 1998-99 a new key performance indicator which seeks "to ensure that 90 per cent of all funds which have a Dedicated Investment Portfolio have a formal investment review at least once a year". This new target replaces the annual and three-year targets described in Figure 16. The Public Trust Office believes that it is more appropriate to have a target whose delivery is within its own control, rather than the current targets which are met or missed according to the performance of the panel brokers against a weighted index of market measures. However, it remains responsible to the Court of Protection for securing the effective investment of patients' funds.

4.17 The one and three-year capital growth targets will still be used for measuring performance on individual portfolios, and performance will continue to be disclosed directly to individual receivers, the Court of Protection and the Honorary Investment Advisory Committee. Unlike the targets it replaces, the new target, which measures performance in reviewing portfolios, is a process rather than an output measure. Although the annual and three-year performance targets will no longer be operated as key performance targets from 1998-99, the Public Trust Office will continue to report publicly performance against these measures as in previous years.

Actual investment performance

4.18 Figure 17 shows the results of actual investment performance since 1994-95. These are discussed below, for cash and portfolios respectively.

Figure 17
Investment performance 1994-95 to 1997-98 against key performance targets

The target for return on cash investments was met for each of the four financial years 1994 to 1998. The target for annual capital performance was missed in 1995-96, 1996-97 and again in 1997-98. The new three year target was missed in 1996-97 and 1997-98.

Type of Investment	Key performance target	1994-95		1995-96		1996-97		1997-98	
		Target (%)	Outturn (%)	Target (%)	Outturn (%)	Target (%)	Outturn (%)	Target (%)	Outturn (%)
Cash	To pay on 'special' rate accounts an annual rate at or above the average of a model set of comparators.	100	Achieved	100	Achieved	100	Achieved	100	Achieved
Portfolios	On an annual basis to ensure that 85% of all measured portfolios perform in line with or better than their model based on market indices.	85	96	85	82.5	85	83	85	67
Portfolios Three-year growth	On a three year rolling basis to ensure that 80% of all measured portfolios perform in line with or better than their model based on market indices.	new target from 1996-97				80	72	80	47

Source: Public Trust Office Annual Reports for 1995-96 to 1997-98

Cash

4.19 In the three years to July 1997, patients' funds in the Accountant General's account with the National Debt Commissioners (Special Account) received interest at a constant eight per cent gross per year. This rate has not been changed since 1993, although the interest rates are regularly reviewed by the Public Trust Office and discussed at the Honorary Investment Advisory Committee. The rate was between two and three per cent higher than the rate patients could have expected to achieve based on the Public Trust Office's model set of high street comparators (Figure 18).

Comparison of rate of interest paid for funds on Special Account with a model set of comparators

Figure 18

In the three years to July 1997, the rate of interest for patients' cash in Special Account was more than two per cent higher than that based on the Public Trust Office's model set of comparators.

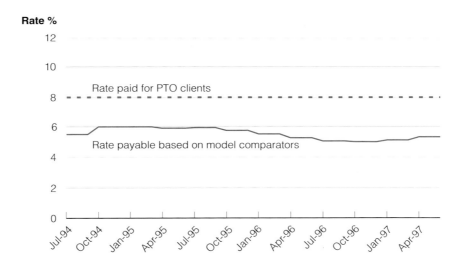

Source: Public Trust Office

Investment portfolios

4.20 In 1994-95, 96 per cent of portfolios achieved a level of annual growth equivalent to 95 per cent of the weighted market index, which was well in excess of the Public Trust Office's target of 85 per cent. Since then, however, targets have not been met (Figure 17). In 1996-97, 83 per cent of portfolios achieved 95 per cent of the growth of the weighted index compared with the 85 per cent target. The three-year target was also not met, with some 72 per cent of portfolios achieving the growth required against the target of 80 per cent (Figure 19). The Public Trust

Office commented in its annual report that dramatic and fluctuating rises in the stockmarket in 1995-96 and 1996-97 meant that any well diversified long-term equity based fund would have found it difficult to keep up with the FTSE 100 index.

Three-year performance of investment portfolios reported during 1996-97

Figure 19

Twenty-eight per cent of portfolios achieved growth below the Public Trust Office's benchmark of 95 per cent of the weighted stock market index and 66 per cent of portfolios achieved growth below the weighted stock market index.

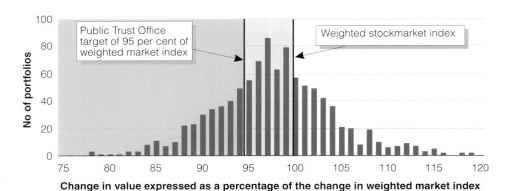

Source: National Audit Office analysis of performance data provided to Public Trust Office by brokers reporting three-year performance comparisons during 1996-97

Notes: Based on 998 portfolios reviewed by the Public Trust Office and included in the three year performance monitoring for 1996-97

4.21 Our study focused on the Public Trust Office's performance up to 1996-97, although we took the opportunity to update our findings where more recent information became available. Investment results for 1997-98 show a substantial deterioration in performance in respect of both the one and three-year capital targets. Only 67 per cent of portfolios achieved the target in respect of one-year performance; performance against the three-year target was worse, at 47 per cent.

4.22 The Public Trust Office told us that the substantial capital gain in United Kingdom equity indices in 1994-98 was concentrated in a limited number of market sectors. To have followed the market in these few exceptional sectors would, it believes, have been in conflict with the requirement of the Court of Protection and the Honorary Investment Advisory Committee that the Public Trust Office should follow a "prudent investor" approach, with long-term diversified portfolios. One of the panel brokers added that it would not have been appropriate to structure a portfolio for which income was an important consideration in a way that exposed it to a small number of specialist sectors. While accepting that investment performance was disappointing, the Public Trust Office pointed out that even those funds which did not reach the Public Trust Office's targets delivered reasonable capital appreciation for patients, and more than enough to match inflation. Case 11 illustrates that investment portfolios that have not met the performance target may still have enjoyed significant capital growth.

Illustrating portfolio growth

Case 11

Mrs G has a large investment portfolio managed by one of the Public Trust Office appointed brokers. Over the three year period to June 1997 the capital growth on her portfolio did not meet the Public Trust Office's target for long-term growth. Nevertheless, the market index relevant to her portfolio rose by 53 per cent during the period, and the capital value of her portfolio rose by 43 per cent. Capital increased in absolute terms from £396,000 to £567,000.

Reviewing performance

4.23 We examined what action the Public Trust Office had taken to identify the reasons for the under-performance on investments noted in Figure 16 and the steps it took to secure improvements.

4.24 Figure 20 shows the different reporting and reviewing requirements for Public Trustee receivership portfolios managed by Public Trust Office staff and those managed by the panel brokers and patients' private brokers. Where portfolios managed by the Public Trust Office's staff or private brokers fall below targets, it aims to review portfolios and consider prompt remedial action. Our examination of a sample of investment portfolios confirmed that this had been done.

4.25 We found that portfolios managed by the panel brokers which failed to meet targets were not always individually reviewed by the Public Trust Office because the broker was expected to follow up with the receiver any changes that might be required. The Public Trust Office also believed that it was important for the broker and the receiver to develop a relationship which allowed the receiver to play a proper part in the management of the patient's capital so that, under professional advice, it could be invested in a way consistent with any expressed wishes of the patient, before they developed mental incapacity.

Figure 20	Arrangements to review investment performance		
	Panel Brokers **(1,468 portfolios)**	**Private Brokers** **(275 portfolios)**	**Public Trust Office Managers** **(901 portfolios)**
Reporting Performance	Annual reports to receiver on performance. One and three-year performance against target reported annually (copied to Public Trust Office).	Annual report to receiver. One and three-year performance against target reported annually (copied to Public Trust Office).	Annual performance reported internally. One and three-year performance against target reported annually.
Public Trust Office review of performance	Public Trust Office monitors broker's overall performance against investment targets every month. Monthly reports to Chief Investment Manager and Management Board. All investments into client funds are collated and the total holdings reviewed by the Honorary Investment Advisory Committee at its meeting following the purchase.	Public Trust Office monitors performance of individual portfolios against investment targets. Monthly reports to Chief Investment Manager and Management Board. All investments into client funds are collated and the total holdings reviewed by the Honorary Investment Advisory Committee at its meeting following the purchase.	Annual performance monitored. Monthly reports to Chief Investment Manager and Management Board. All investments into client funds are collated and the total holdings reviewed by the Honorary Investment Advisory Committee at its meeting following the purchase.
Action on under- performing portfolios	The Public Trust Office seeks to ensure that the panel brokers are transparent in their explanations of individual poor performance. It may pursue more detailed explanations in exceptional cases. If a broker's global performance gives cause for concern, the Public Trust Office may raise the matter with Honorary Investment Advisory Committee on the recommendation of the Chief Investment Manager.	Broker has to provide written explanation to receiver for under-performing portfolios. Public Trust Office should request explanation if none is offered or if the explanation is inadequate.	Investment Manager provides written explanation of reasons for under-performance to Senior Investment Manager along with remedial proposals.
National Audit Office examination	One broker performed satisfactorily. The other broker was challenged to explain its performance which led to two appearances before the Honorary Investment Advisory Committee. The Committee required considerable analysis of the situation by the broker and doubled the number of performance returns in order to monitor the broker more closely.	We examined 20 per cent of under-performing portfolios, ranging from 12 to 14 per cent below target growth. The Public Trust Office had asked for explanations in all cases.	We examined 20 per cent of under-performing portfolios, ranging from 6 to 13 per cent below target growth. Of these, the Public Trust Office had provided explanations or proposals for changes in investments in every case.

Source: National Audit Office

4.26 The Public Trust Office does, however, monitor comparative performance for capital growth achieved by the panel brokers across all the portfolios for which they are responsible. Figure 21 shows the relative performance of the panel brokers, private brokers and Public Trust Office staff, against the one-year capital growth target. More than three-quarters of the private receivership portfolios which failed to achieve the one-year target growth in 1996-97 were managed by one of the two panel brokers, James Capel Investment Management. This poor performance against the target first came to the Public Trust Office's attention in July 1995.

Figure 21	**Performance of investment managers against the one-year capital growth target for 1996-97 and the three-year target 1994-95 to 1996-97**

The Public Trust Office's decision to terminate one broker's contract reflected performance on capital growth relative to the targets set, which did not take account of income earned on investments.

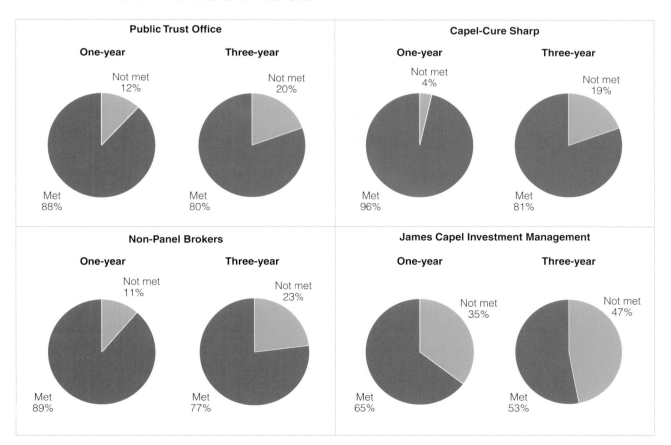

Note: The Public Trust Office regards the three-year target as more indicative of a portfolio's capital performance than the one-year target, because the three-year target was predicated on a minimum five-year investment life

Source: Public Trust Office records for portfolios monitored during 1996-97

4.27 Figure 21 also shows relative performance against the three-year capital growth target. Almost half of the measured portfolios managed by James Capel Investment Management failed to meet the target. These patients may have enjoyed higher investment income at the expense of capital growth, but the Public Trust Office does not have global management information on income. It considered that since the broker had already reported the income and capital growth individually to each receiver, further monitoring of income would be inconclusive and would involve unnecessary expense for patients. It also felt that not all the information needed for such monitoring would be available from every investment advisor appointed by the Court of Protection.

4.28 With the co-operation of James Capel Investment Management, the Public Trust Office explored the broker's relative under-performance against the capital targets, and examined information on the shares held in the portfolios that the broker managed. The broker told us that they continued to structure those portfolios requiring a focus on income as far as possible to meet the specified income requirements of patients, though without including some high growth but less predictable sectors which boosted the overall performance of the stockmarket. The Public Trust Office pointed out that each panel broker had the same proportion of patients, 40 per cent, who required an emphasis on income rather than capital growth. It therefore considered that it was legitimate to compare the relative performance of both brokers against the capital targets.

4.29 Over the following year, there was no significant improvement in James Capel Investment Management's relative performance against the capital targets and in July 1996, the broker was required to provide a formal explanation to the Lord Chancellor's Honorary Investment Advisory Committee. The broker promised to review all portfolios individually and to allocate additional resources to the team working on the contract with the Public Trust Office.

4.30 The Honorary Investment Advisory Committee agreed with James Capel Investment Management that some portfolios needed to be re-structured in order to change the emphasis in line with the capital targets, and the broker was asked to address this on all subsequent portfolio reviews. All transactions were approved in advance by the receivers and reviewed in retrospect by the Honorary Investment Advisory Committee. While accepting that the restructuring would take time to implement, for example to take account of tax considerations, and incur additional costs for the patients, the Public Trust Office and James Capel Investment Management believed that it offered the chance to improve the future performance of patients' portfolios against the one and three-year capital targets.

4.31 The overall commission earned by James Capel Investment Management remained constant from 1995-96 to 1997-98 at 0.276 per cent of the total value of funds under their management. The commission of the other panel broker declined as a percentage of funds under their management from 0.263 per cent in 1995-96, through 0.228 per cent in 1996-97, to 0.16 per cent in 1997-98, reflecting the level of activity they considered necessary during these years when the market was rising. The Public Trust Office believes that the commission charged by both brokers represents good value for money for the services received, as set out in paragraph 4.10.

4.32 At the April 1997 meeting of the Honorary Investment Advisory Committee, the Court of Protection asked the Committee whether James Capel Investment Management's commission rates could be renegotiated. The Public Trust Office confirmed that in theory this could be done. However, the Committee felt that higher than average commission was inevitable while the restructuring was in progress. The Public Trust Office did not seek legal opinion as to whether James Capel Investment Management was contractually entitled to charge commission for the restructuring on the grounds that there was no clear definition of what restructuring entailed. It did not separately record which portfolios the broker restructured because of the difficulty of establishing whether any sale or purchase of shares was part of the restructuring process or the ongoing management of the portfolio. For example, a sale of an under-performing share might be described as either restructuring or as good portfolio management. A sale might also involve patients' original holdings not purchased by James Capel Investment Management.

4.33 The broker put considerable effort into the restructuring, but the Public Trust Office judged that there was a further deterioration in the administration and investment performance of James Capel Investment Management measured against the Public Trust Office's capital targets and relative to the capital performance achieved by the other broker. In November 1997, the Public Trust Office gave the company notice that it intended to terminate its contract on 20 March 1998. Appendix 5 sets out a full timetable of the events leading to the termination of contract.

Recommendation 17

The Public Trust Office should ensure that there is a sufficiently robust system in place for monitoring panel brokers which would prompt early and effective action where there is evidence of poor performance.

4.34 A competitive tendering exercise was held in early 1998 to replace the panel broker. For reasons of cost efficiency only, to enable simultaneous competitive tendering for both contracts, the contract of the other panel broker,

Capel-Cure Sharp, was also terminated. Capel-Cure Sharp was successful in retendering for the contract. Brewin Dolphin Securities was appointed as the other panel broker.

4.35 Before the new contracts were let, we suggested to the Public Trust Office that it should consider incorporating in the contracts performance targets clearly linked to its own corporate targets. In the event, the Public Trust Office decided not to incorporate the targets into the contracts as fundamental terms. It considered that the targets would impair the brokers' flexibility to deal with fluctuating markets and the complex circumstances of individual patients, where failure to meet the targets for individual portfolios might be acceptable. However, it alerted the new brokers to the performance it expected from them.

Part 5: Financial management

5.1   In 1994 we reported a widespread perception that Public Trust Office fees were high. The Committee of Public Accounts looked to the Public Trust Office to make significant financial savings without jeopardising the interests of patients and to reduce subsidisation of some patients by fees charged to others.

5.2   A pre-condition of successful financial management, and for an appropriate charging regime, is the existence of proper accounts prepared in accordance with generally accepted accounting practice in so far as appropriate, and Government Accounting requirements. This part of the report examines the financial management of the Public Trust Office and in particular the progress it has made in:

- producing improved accounts;

- reducing costs and improving efficiency; and

- reducing the cross-subsidisation of Public Trustee receivership patients by private receivership patients.

Progress in producing improved accounts

5.3   The Public Trust Office, which was established as an executive agency on 1 July 1994, reports on financial performance in its annual report but its financial statements recording the costs, income and financial position of the agency are currently unaudited. Audited accounts are produced annually for Funds held in Court (based on a year to 28 February).

5.4   Guidance issued by the Treasury requires that agencies should produce audited accounts from launch, and, where this is not possible, accounting systems should be improved to produce audited accruals accounts covering the second full year of operation. In July 1994, the Public Trust Office did not have appropriate systems in place to support the new accounting requirements. With the installation of a new accruals accounting system from 1 April 1996 the intention was to produce auditable financial statements for 1996-97, the second full year of operation. The 1996-97 financial statements would be drawn up on an accruals basis, whereby income earned is matched with expenditure incurred. Financial statements prepared on such a basis would provide consistent information on which to assess financial performance and, when audited, provide assurance on the material accuracy of the amounts included. They would be of use both to the Public Trust Office for financial planning and to those interested in its performance.

Financial reporting requirements

5.5 We carried out a preliminary assessment of the Public Trust Office's accounting systems and policies during the 1996-97 financial year. Subsequently, the Public Trust Office agreed with us that it was not in a position to produce full accruals accounts for 1996-97 to a standard that would be likely to receive an unqualified audit certificate from the Comptroller and Auditor General, although the Public Trust Office expected to be in a position to prepare such accounts for 1997-98. We therefore examined the accounts included in the 1996-97 annual report as a basis for identifying the improvements necessary to allow the production of commercial-style accounts to the required standard for 1997-98. Our examination included consideration of whether the accounting policies applied were appropriate to meet the requirements of accruals accounting and whether systems and procedures were sufficiently robust to identify all relevant transactions and treat them appropriately.

Reliability of the Public Trust Office's published accounts

5.6 Published accounts produced by the Public Trust Office for 1996-97 showed an operating surplus of £4,000. As a result of our examination, we identified a number of deficiencies and estimate that the net monetary impact of these resulted initially in a deficit of £72,000 and then, following a late adjustment for Value Added Tax, a surplus of £19,000 (Figure 22). However, we consider that uncertainties about the robustness of data included in the accounting records mean that the results are unreliable.

5.7 We found a number of fundamental systems and procedural weaknesses which affect the Public Trust Office's ability to produce accounts on an accruals basis. Given the scale of these problems, the Public Trust Office has determined that it will not be in a position to produce audited accruals accounts for 1997-98 as it had expected.

Revised income and expenditure account for the year ended 31 March 1997

Figure 22

Showing an extract of the Public Trust Office's published unaudited income and expenditure account for the year ended 31 March 1997, with adjustments to take account of a Value Added Tax recovery identified subsequently (paragraph 5.9). The second column shows our estimate of the Public Trust Office's results for 1996-97 following our examination of the published figures.

	Public Trust Office's Unaudited Figures £000	NAO Estimated Figures £000
Total income	19,278	19,586
Total expenditure	19,274	19,658
Operating surplus/(deficit)	4	(72)
Add adjustment for Value Added Tax identified following publication of the 1996-97 accounts	91	91
Operating surplus/(deficit) following adjustment for Value Added Tax	95	19
Full cost recovery per published accounts (per cent)	100.0	99.6
Full cost recovery following adjustment for Value Added Tax (per cent)	100.5	100.1

Source: Public Trust Office Annual Report for 1996-97 and National Audit Office examination of financial statements

5.8 The issues identified from our examination are in summary:

■ errors on private receivership fee income, including fee adjustments recorded in the wrong year of account which, whilst netting out to have negligible monetary impact on the 1996-97 operating results, cast doubt on the underlying integrity of the records;

■ errors on Public Trustee receivership fee income, including fee adjustments recorded in the wrong year of account, for which the monetary impact has not been estimated since initial audit results revealed problems similar to those for private receivership fee income;

■ accrued fee income omitted from the balance sheet and the likelihood that fee debtors in the agency account are also understated; and

■ errors on expenditure and income items, including those which directly affect the figures included in the published accounts but which have no impact on the recorded surplus.

We concluded that the Public Trust Office was not in a position to produce robust financial data. The uncertainties about the accuracy of recorded information means that only limited reliance can be placed on the data contained in the Public Trust Office's published 1996-97 financial statements. One implication is that the level of bonus paid to the Chief Executive of the Public Trust Office cannot be fully and independently validated, because it is partly based on financial data. Such validation is required by Treasury guidance contained in "Next Steps Agencies: Annual Report and Accounts", issued in 1993. Independent validation was also recommended by the Committee of Public Accounts in their report on *the Meteorological Office Executive Agency: Evaluation of Performance* (HC279, Session 1995-96), and accepted in the subsequent Treasury Minute.

5.9 As shown in Figure 22, inclusion in the Public Trust Office's published figures of a recovery of Value Added Tax for the fourth quarter of 1996-97 totalling £91,000 would have increased the published surplus, as calculated by the Public Trust Office, to £95,000. The Public Trust Office was not in a position to identify this amount until December 1997, nor confirm the relevance of the total VAT recoveries which should have been reflected in the 1996-97 year of account until August 1998. VAT recoveries for the Public Trust Office are administered centrally by the Lord Chancellor's Department. Our examination identified the need for the Public Trust Office to ensure that VAT recoveries can be accurately recorded and promptly received.

5.10 Comparisons with previous years' accounts are affected by inconsistencies in the accounting treatments applied since the Public Trust Office acquired executive agency status. In particular the level of debts collected in 1996-97 relating to prior years (discussed further in paragraph 5.20), suggests that income statements in previous years were materially incomplete. This makes meaningful comparisons of financial performance based on information in the statements difficult.

Recommendation 18 | The Public Trust Office should draw up an action plan to review all appropriate fee accounts, identify debts outstanding and establish material accruals, along with a timetable for the production of auditable accounts for 1998-99.

Treatment of income in calculating Mental Health Sector fees

Fee raising procedures

5.11 In line with the Fees Order, annual fees are raised on the latest information about the patient's clear annual income. However, these remain estimates until the receiver's account is received and reviewed. As indicated in Part 2 of this report, the Public Trust Office's aims are as follows:

- private receivers should lodge their annual account within one month of the anniversary date of the case. The Public Trust Office then aims to review 80 per cent of these cases within four weeks of receipt; and

- Public Trustee receivership accounts are produced annually, and checked either annually or biannually depending on the Public Trust Office's assessment of the risk involved in each case, and should be reviewed within eight weeks of the due date.

5.12 The accounts review is a key element of the fee raising and income collection process, and for Public Trustee receivership cases provides an essential control over caseworkers' action in this respect. In addition to calculating the final annual fee, the review includes a check on the accuracy and quality of the work carried out by Public Trust Office caseworkers and private receivers. If the final fee calculation differs from the estimated fee already charged, the reviewing branch adjusts the fee directly or, for Public Trustee receiverships, instructs the patient's caseworker to make the adjustment. This action should result in either an additional amount being collected, or a refund being made to the patient's account. The reviewing branch also instructs the caseworker, for Public Trustee receiverships, to correct any errors in the handling of patients' transactions identified from the review, or notifies the private receiver of any errors found in the accuracy of their work. Such errors may affect the accuracy of the patient's clear annual income on which the fee is based.

5.13 The accurate, timely and complete calculation and recording of private receivership fees may be adversely affected by the late or non-submission of patients' accounts by private receivers, and any delays in review once these are received. Similarly, inappropriate fee levels may be applied to those Public Trustee receiverships for those accounts which are determined by the Public Trust Office for review only every two years. These delays affect both the timing of adjustments to past fees, and the correction of fees being collected now and in the future.

5.14 We examined actions relating to 1996-97 fees for a sample of 115 private receivership and 43 Public Trustee receivership cases and found that:

- 32 per cent of Public Trustee receivership cases and 24 per cent of private receivership cases, where fees were due in 1996-97, had not been reviewed either during the financial year or in the period up to the end of August 1997; and

- in 12 per cent of private receivership cases, accounts had not been received or reviewed for between one and three years prior to their 1996-97 financial year anniversary date. In most cases there was no evidence on file of regular reminders to private receivers. As a consequence, no formal review of private receiver action had taken place in that time on those cases.

5.15 In some other cases, we found that reviews had taken place after several years of absent accounts but corrective fee action was not fully implemented. Incorrect treatments arising from the review process included duplicate fees raised and duplicate refunds issued on fee adjustments. We also noted errors in the transactions handled on behalf of Public Trustee patients. These shortcomings sometimes resulted in sizeable errors on patients' individual accounts (Cases 12 and 13).

Delay in the collection and subsequent over-collection

Case 12

A patient suffering from senile dementia was the subject of a private receivership from December 1994. The 1994-95 account was reviewed in January 1996 and the first annual fee calculated as £216. The amount was collected from funds held in court in two parts, in January and February 1996.

A fee of £200 based on the patient's second account was raised three times, twice incorrectly, and taken from the patient's funds in March 1997. One of the overpayments was identified by review and refunded in June 1997. The second overpayment had not been identified or refunded at the time of our examination, but was subsequently corrected on the patient's death in February 1998.

Delay in the collection and subsequent over-collection

Case 13

An elderly patient suffering from dementia was the subject of a private receivership from June 1986. In 1992, following the receiver's failure to submit five consecutive sets of annual accounts, the Public Trustee was appointed receiver. A review in April 1996 of the patient's account to July 1995 revealed several errors by the caseworker. These included:

- the duplicate payment of a £150 appointment fee (corrected in March 1997);
- a duplicate payment of nursing fees of £1,303 which was identified and notified for correction by the payee;
- the failure to collect the £100 commencement fee; and
- an incorrect claim for income support later corrected by another caseworker.

This review also showed that the fee band of £1,300 was too high and should be reduced to £800, with a corresponding need to refund the patient £400 and £500 for fees paid in 1994 and 1995 respectively.

A review in September 1996 of the accounts to September 1996 showed that the fee band had not in fact been changed and that a further £1,200 refund was required as £1,300 had again been charged for 1996, when the correct fee was by then £100.

We found that the refunds of £400 and £500 had been refunded twice, in October 1996 and in March 1997. We also noted that the fee band had still not been changed and that a further £1,300 had been charged to the patient for annual fees for 1997.

5.16 The errors in accurate recording of fees on Public Trustee receiverships arose in part because instructions on fees had either been incorrectly actioned or not actioned at all by the patient's caseworker. There are formal procedures for actioning changes to fees, but where caseworkers fail to implement changes correctly, the error or omission may continue until the next account review.

Impact on accounting records

5.17 Our sample examination of patients' cases also revealed a high level of undetected error in the recording of fees on the accruals accounting system. In our sample of cases, we found that 31 per cent of private receivership fees and 42 per cent of annual Public Trustee receivership fees due in 1996-97 had not been recorded correctly. These errors included, for example, fee adjustments recorded in the wrong year of account, fees due but not raised or raised in duplicate, and mis-postings to the accounting system.

5.18 We estimate that the gross impact of the various errors identified from our statistical evaluation of the 115 private receivership cases reviewed is some £1.3 million in relation to this source of 1996-97 income alone. This amount includes errors which understate and overstate the value of recorded fee income to a similar degree, with the result that the net monetary impact on reported private receivership income of £8.676 million for 1996-97 happens to be negligible, although errors may be significant for individual patients. The errors distort the information available to management, and the Public Trust Office may not therefore collect promptly, or at all, the fees due to it.

Recommendation 19	The Public Trust Office should ensure that fee adjustments and errors in fee calculation are identified and are addressed promptly.

Debtor identification and debt management

5.19 Our sample of cases showed that the average time taken to complete fee collection procedures for fees due in 1996-97 was at least 232 days for Public Trustee receiverships, and at least 258 days for private receiverships. A fee is due on the anniversary date of a case. The average of at least 232 days for Public Trustee receiverships is partly a consequence of the Public Trust Office's approach of reviewing some cases every two years according to their risk assessment (paragraph 5.11). During this time the relevant fee income may not be recorded accurately in the accounting records.

5.20 Prior to the installation of a new accruals accounting system on 1 April 1996, the Public Trust Office did not have any centralised accounting information, or reliable centralised management information about the level of patient fee debt. The Public Trust Office recognised the need to identify the level of outstanding fees for the 1996-97 accounts, including fees due but not raised in years prior to 1996-97. During 1996-97, the Public Trust Office undertook an exercise to record debts outstanding on each case on the accruals accounting system, and to collect the amounts due from previous years. The review found that at least £2.298 million of private receivership fees and £124,000 of Public Trustee receivership fees relating to years prior to 1996-97 had neither been raised at 31 March 1997 nor collected before the 1996-97 financial year; nor had amounts been recorded in previous unaudited accounts. The review also estimated that a further £282,000 of income had not been raised at 31 March 1997 on cases that were in the process of being wound up, but since not all cases were reviewed this may be an underestimate. The Public Trust Office's own review therefore confirmed that a significant balance of fees had not been raised or collected on a timely basis in the past. Our review of income systems also casts doubt on the completeness and accuracy of the fees recorded.

Recommendation 20	The Public Trust Office should establish the correct fee position for debts and current fees for all cases and amend accounting records accordingly.

5.21 The accruals system implemented in 1996 should enable central monitoring of amounts collected against those recorded as due, but this record will not be effective so long as the significant weaknesses in the underlying procedures for raising fees for receiverships persist. We consider that until these weaknesses are resolved, the Public Trust Office will be unable to monitor fee collection effectively, or to demonstrate that the income and debtors included in the published accounts are complete.

Recommendation 21

The Public Trust Office should establish and implement a comprehensive income policy to cover the raising, recording, review and collection of fee income from receivership patients, with clear responsibilities for all stages in the process and appropriate management controls to monitor compliance with the policy.

Accounting policy for income

5.22 The Public Trust Office's accounting policy for annual fees is to recognise them in full in the year in which they are raised, and to recognise fee adjustments in the year in which they are made. This policy was employed in reflection of the working practices and management information systems in place at the time agency status was granted. The Public Trust Office considered these policies to be in line with those of the Lord Chancellor's Department group accounting policies, although these have not been agreed with the National Audit Office, and the chargeable services provided by the Department are not necessarily comparable to those of the Public Trust Office. The new accruals accounting system installed in April 1996 was specified to meet the requirement of these policies. The Public Trust Office considers that the policy applied ensures that there is a sufficiently close relationship between fee income and expenditure overall.

5.23 However, generally accepted accounting practice requires income to be matched to expenditure within an accounting period. The Public Trust Office's accounting policy for income does not therefore meet generally accepted accounting practice as fee income is not matched to the expenditure incurred in managing the receivership over the period to which the fee relates. In many cases fee adjustments have been recorded as income in the wrong year of account. Thus, where income for 1996-97 is not raised until 1997-98, a fair value is not placed on the related work carried out during 1996-97. Based on the extrapolated results of our case review examination, the value of this accrued income at 31 March 1997 is estimated at £3,410,000 for private receiverships and £1,246,000 for Public Trustee receiverships. This is wrongly excluded from the balance sheet. There is no estimate of accrued income at 1 April 1996, which, if shown, the Public Trust Office considers would be of a broadly similar amount.

5.24 Until this matter is resolved, the Public Trust Office will not be able to prepare accounts which meet accruals requirements, nor will they derive the benefits of the commercial-style of accounting expected of an executive agency. The implementation of accruals based accounting, including the recognition of accrued income, would strengthen the information produced by management and highlight any continuing problems with the control of income and debtors. The ability to identify fees in accruals terms is linked closely with the underlying need for the Public Trust Office to put in place adequate procedures to completely and accurately collect fees on a timely basis. The Public Trust Office is now in the process of revising the accounting policy so that it will be able to derive the benefits of the more demanding commercial-style of accounting expected of an executive agency. We consider that once income systems are properly controlled, the additional procedures required to apply generally accepted accounting practice for recognising income will not be significant.

Procedures for including relevant expenditure in the accounts

5.25 The Public Trust Office had established year-end accounting procedures which were not sufficiently robust and, as a consequence, material costs were included in the wrong year of account or excluded from expenditure. The main errors, which arise from a review of expenditure in respect of all activities in the published statements, including that for the Trust and Court Funds services, are shown in Figure 23.

5.26 In our estimate of the Public Trust Office's 1996-97 results shown in Figure 22, we included the adjustments required to correct the errors in relation to expenditure. We also included additional notional costs of £284,000 arising from capital charges attributable to amounts estimated for accrued income which would not be invoiced until 1997-98. The overall result of these adjustments was to increase the Public Trust Office's reported income and expenditure by £308,000 and £384,000 respectively, resulting in a deficit on operations of £72,000 or a surplus of £19,000 following the late adjustment for Value Added Tax (paragraph 5.9). The Public Trust Office needs to establish more robust procedures to ensure that all material transactions are recognised appropriately in the accounts.

Recommendation 22

The Public Trust Office should introduce adequate procedures for identifying year end accruals and for applying the appropriate accounting treatment to all material transactions.

Overstatements and understatements of expenditure, 1996-97

Source: National Audit Office examination of Public Trust Office financial statements

Figure 23

Overstatements reflecting amounts which were included incorrectly as 1996-97 expenditure:

■ £175,000 in respect of goods and services paid in 1996-97 but relevant to 1997-98;

■ £83,000 of invoices received and paid in 1996-97 for goods and services, but relevant to 1995-96; and

■ other miscellaneous amounts of £8,000 included incorrectly as 1996-97 expenditure.

Understatements reflecting amounts which were omitted incorrectly from 1996-97 expenditure:

■ £84,000 of invoices received and paid in 1997-98 for goods and services, but relevant to 1996-97; and

■ £109,000 of invoices received and paid in 1995-96 in respect of goods and services, but relevant to 1996-97.

Amounts which understate recorded expenditure and income to the same degree, whilst having no impact on the surplus/deficit for the year:

■ special payments and cash losses totalling £80,000 and the associated credit from the Lord Chancellor's Department to finance these costs; and

■ £280,000 in fees which were waived where patients did not have sufficient funds to meet them, where payment would have caused financial hardship, or on Trusts, where the work was deemed exceptionally simple.

Progress in reducing costs and improving efficiency

5.27 The cost of administering and monitoring receiverships in 1996-97 was approximately £11.5 million. Prior to 1997-98, the Public Trust Office measured efficiency using a weighted mean percentage reduction in costs, representing the cost of dealing with an average case in the main areas of business, including receiverships. The use of such a measure requires delivery of overall savings, without expecting all divisions to meet the target. In 1994, the Public Trust Office made a commitment to the Committee of Public Accounts to seek to reduce unit costs by two per cent in real terms each year for three years. This implied an overall decrease in real terms in both costs and fees charged to patients.

5.28 The Public Trust Office measures its annual performance against a target for efficiency saving agreed with the Lord Chancellor's Department. This target is set in relation to the previous year's target. The Public Trust Office reported that it had met the target for efficiency savings for the organisation as a whole in each of the three financial years ending in 1996-97.

5.29 The usefulness of unit costs as a measure of efficiency depends to a great extent on the accuracy, completeness and reliability of the two constituent elements – the units of work and the costs of the different types of work. We have concerns about the reliability of the unit cost calculations, because, in the absence of independently audited accounts there can be only limited assurance that the available financial statements provide consistent and complete information on which to assess financial performance, or that the amounts included are materially accurate. In view of the absence of independently audited accounts since the Public Trust Office became an executive agency in July 1994, we have concluded that it is not possible to confirm that the Public Trust Office met its targets agreed with the Lord Chancellor's Department, or its 1994 commitment to the Committee of Public Accounts to reduce unit costs by two per cent in real terms each year for three years.

5.30 Caseload data used in the calculation, which are derived from the Public Trust Office's case recording system, are highly aggregated. For example, private receivership cases are grouped as 34,000 cases, whereas there are 19,500 current receiverships, 6,500 applications for receiverships and 8,000 receiverships which are in the process of being wound up. The high level of aggregation of caseload reduces the value of unit costs as a measure of efficiency, because differing levels of efficiency achieved for distinct types of work are masked when combined into a single measure.

Recommendation 23

The Public Trust Office, with the assistance of the Lord Chancellor's Department, should ensure it has in place arrangements to provide independent validation of its efficiency savings.

Recommendation 24

The Public Trust Office should differentiate costs and caseload data to a lower level so that efficiencies and inefficiencies of different types of work can be identified.

5.31 The Public Trust Office does not collect information on the time its staff spend on individual cases. Such information would allow the costs of the different tasks to be more accurately determined, for example processing applications, monitoring receivership accounts, supervising patients' investments and winding up receiverships. Introducing a system to record time on casework would involve start-up and continuing costs. The information would help management to allocate resources effectively.

5.32 To work efficiently, a time-recording system would need to be supported by a computerised case management system. In 1994, consultants considered that the introduction of such a system was "essential" for the efficient management of the receivership caseload. The recommendation was accepted but has not yet been implemented owing to significant cost considerations and because other information technology projects have higher priorities and, in the case of Year 2000 compliance, immovable deadlines.

Recommendation 25	The Public Trust Office should consider including in its Information Systems Strategy a time-recording system that will allow it to cost accurately the time spent monitoring and administering receiverships.

Cross-subsidisation

5.33 The Government's policy is that there should be no public subsidy of receivership work. The Public Trust Office therefore aims to recover the costs of receiverships through fees. Current fee rates are set out in Figure 24 and came into force in December 1994. Since April 1995, patients with private receivers have been charged, on average, five per cent of their clear annual income. Public Trustee patients have been charged approximately 20 per cent of their clear annual income in annual fees, reflecting the greater amount of work involved in administering the receivership. Approximately one-third of Public Trustee receivership patients are liable for the minimum fee of £100 as their assessable income is less than £1,000, and there is provision for the fee to be remitted on grounds of hardship.

5.34 We found two kinds of cross-subsidy, although as the Public Trust Office does not know the cost of managing or monitoring individual cases, this has to remain only a broad indication of the relationship between fees charged and income received.

■ Using the Public Trust Office's average weighted unit cost per case, patients with higher income levels pay more in fees than the Public Trust Office's average costs in administering the receivership, whilst those with lower levels of income pay less than the average cost of administering the receivership. For both private and Public Trustee receiverships a subsidy has to operate where fees are waived on grounds of financial hardship.

■ The total fee income from Public Trustee patients is insufficient to cover the much higher costs associated with these receiverships. The balance is met from fees charged to private receivership patients. At the time of our previous examination, more than half of the costs of the work done on behalf of Public Trustee receivership patients was being met by private receivership patients. By 1997 this had fallen to 37 per cent.

Fee bands for annual administration fees and average costs per patient

Figure 24

The administration fee charged to Public Trustee patients is considerably higher than those charged to private receivership patients, reflecting the greater workload involved in Public Trustee cases.

Clear annual income[1]		Annual fee	
		Public Trustee receivership	**Private receivership**
Fee Band	**Income range £**	**Fee £**	**Fee £**
1	0-999	100	50
2	1,000-1,999	250	70
3	2,000-2,999	525	130
4	3,000-4,999	800	200
5	5,000-6,999	1,300	350
6	7,000-9,999	1,800	550
7	10,000-15,000	2,800	800
8	over 15,000	2,800[2]	800[2]

Notes: 1 Clear annual income is calculated as the total income at the patient's disposal in the year of administration less allowable deductions such as non-taxable benefit payments, bank charges and a part of any awards for damages received.

2 Fees for Band 8 are charged at the rate for Band 7 plus five per cent of income exceeding £15,000.

3 The Public Trust Office's average weighted unit costs for handling work are £1,350 per patient for Public Trustee receiverships and £195 per patient for private receiverships.

Source: Public Trust Office

5.35 The Committee of Public Accounts expressed concern about the cross-subsidy between Public Trustee and private receiverships. The Committee considered it unacceptable that private receivership patients should have to pay for services which they were not receiving, and expected the Public Trust Office to reduce the subsidy. The Public Trust Office subsequently set a target to reduce the level of cross-subsidy from 52 per cent in 1993-94 to 30 per cent of Public Trustee receivership costs by 1996-97. In 1994, the Court of Protection set new fee rates which increased all the rates charged to Public Trustee patients, whilst reducing the majority of rates charged to private receivership patients (Figure 25). As a result, the subsidy of Public Trustee patients by private receivership patients fell, but did not meet the 30 per cent target (Figure 26).

Changes in fee rates charged to Public Trustee and private receivership patients since 1993-94

Figure 25

New fee rates introduced by the 1994 Court of Protection Rules reduced private receivership fees in all but the lowest income band and increased the fees for all Public Trustee receiverships.

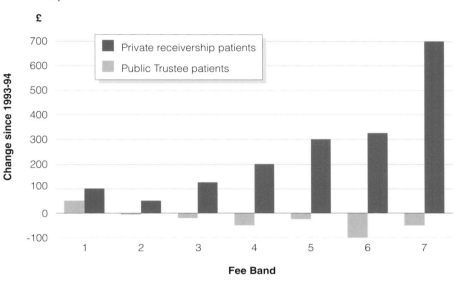

Source: Public Trust Office Fee Bands 1993-94 and 1996-97

Note: Fee rates were increased once in the period, with effect from 1 April 1995

Cross-subsidy of Public Trustee receivership patients by private receivership patients 1994-95 to 1997-98

Figure 26

The Public Trust Office has reduced the level of cross-subsidy but did not meet the target for a reduction to 30 per cent by 1996-97. The subsidy was further reduced to 32 per cent in 1997-98.

Percentage level of subsidy

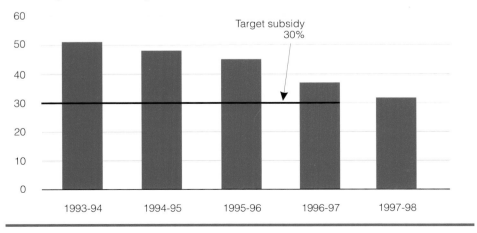

Source: Public Trust Office Annual Report and Accounts

5.36 The deficit on Public Trustee receivership work is now around £1.5 million a year. Ministers considered that reducing the cross-subsidy to zero through higher fees to Public Trustee receivership patients would be unacceptable as it would require fees for those patients to be raised to an exorbitant level. They therefore endorsed the approach of subsidising Public Trustee receivership patients by higher fees charged to private receivership patients. The direct impact of the cross-subsidy is that private receivership patients are, in total, continuing to pay on average 21 per cent more than the cost of the services delivered to them to fund the unrecovered costs of work on Public Trustee receiverships.

Part 6: Customer service

6.1 In 1994, we reported the results of our survey of receivers and carers on the quality of customer service provided by the Public Trust Office. In the light of the results, we suggested that it could improve its service to users by:

■ establishing standards of service;

■ providing clearer information for prospective receivers;

■ providing greater continuity of contacts with receivers and carers;

■ standardising responses to enquiries from users and members of the public;

■ obtaining the views of clients on the quality of service provided;

■ establishing more rigorous complaints procedures; and

■ enhancing the skills and expertise of staff to help them deliver improved services.

This part of the report examines the progress the Public Trust Office has made in these areas.

Establishing standards of service

6.2 Since becoming an executive agency in 1994, the Public Trust Office has published service standards which set out what the public can expect of it and its staff. There are separate standards relating to the work on private receivership cases, based partly on those expected of all government departments under the Citizen's Charter, and partly on the Public Trust Office's assessment of what clients additionally consider important. In summer 1998, the Public Trust Office carried out a client survey to obtain views on the relevance and importance of each of its standards of service and is currently analysing the results.

6.3 Figures 27 and 28 show the standards and performance against targets for 1996-97. The Public Trust Office's aim is a 98 per cent achievement for each service standard. For private receiverships and Enduring Powers of Attorney, this target was achieved for two of the 11 standards only. For Public Trustee receiverships, the target was achieved for three out of the 11 standards. This level of performance was similar to that achieved in 1994-95 and 1995-96. The two standards met in 1996-97 for private receiverships related to notifications sent to customers acknowledging receipt of applications, and to the validation and onward transmission of documents. While performance against both of these targets contributes to the quality of service received by customers, we do not believe they are the most important of the Public Trust Office's customer service targets. For example, it seems to us that the timeliness target for issuing a court order setting up a receivership is likely to be more important than the timing of acknowledging applications to set up a receiverships.

6.4 The Public Trust Office regards replying to correspondence, standard 1, as particularly important because of the volume of work that it covers and because it is a national standard. In 1996-97, the Public Trust Office fell slightly below the target of 98 per cent for standard 1, achieving 95 per cent for private receiverships and Enduring Powers of Attorney (paragraphs 2.30 to 2.35), and 93 per cent for Public Trustee receiverships.

6.5 The Public Trust Office does not prioritise its standards to ensure that staff effort is concentrated on any individual element of its work. The Law Society told us that the professional receivers it represents were particularly concerned to have a prompt and efficient service in respect of standards 5, 6 and 7 in Figure 27. However, the Public Trust Office's performance against these standards in 1996-97 was the lowest recorded. The Law Society also highlighted the time taken by the Public Trust Office to review and pass receivers' accounts. This was also a major concern of the Committee of Public Accounts (Appendix 2, items 1 and 2), but no customer service standards are set for this element of the Public Trust Office's work.

Service standards for private receiverships and Enduring Powers of Attorney

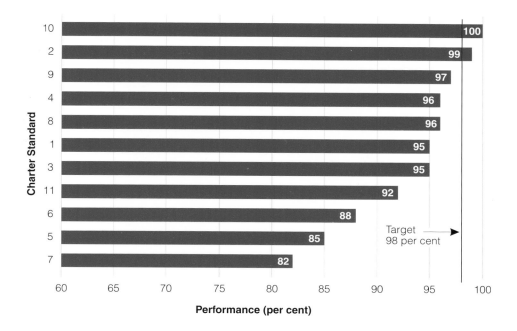

Figure 27

In 1996-97, the Public Trust Office achieved its target customer service performance in two out of its 11 service targets for private receiverships and Enduring Powers of Attorney.

1. Letters responded to within 10 working days or acknowledged within three working days and responded to within 20 working days.
2. Applications for the registration of an Enduring Power of Attorney acknowledged within three working days.
3. Enduring Powers of Attorney registered and returned within five working days of the completion of the 35 day waiting period or information sent to clients of any problems or objections to registration.
4. Applications for a First General Order (FGO) acknowledged within three working days of receipt.
5. Draft First General Orders sent out within eight weeks of the application being issued or the client informed of any problems or objections during this period.
6. Sealed copies of FGO sent within four weeks of return of the draft order in cases where all matters raised by the Court of Protection have been dealt with.
7. Directions sent to receivers within 10 working days of request for money (not held by Court Funds Office), or notification sent within this period that the request was not approved.
8. Directions sent to Court Funds Office to release money held within 10 working days of request, or notification sent that the request was not approved.
9. Complaints to Heads of Division responded to within 15 working days.
10. Grants of Probate/Letters of Administration sent to Personal Representatives within three working days of receipt.
11. Directions to transfer assets held by Court Funds Office prepared within four weeks of receipt of grant of representation.

Source: Public Trust Office

Service standards for Public Trustee receiverships

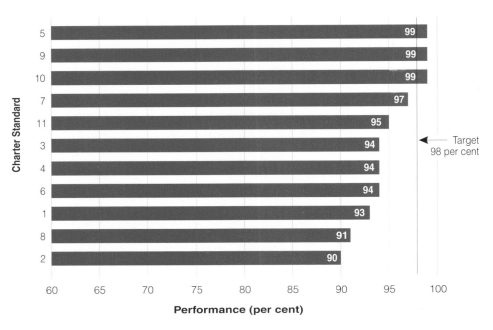

Figure 28

In 1996-97, the Public Trust Office achieved its target customer service performance in three out of its 11 service targets for Public Trustee receiverships.

1. Letters responded to within 10 working days or acknowledged within three working days and responded to within 20 working days.
2. Cases where client notified of Public Trust Office involvement within three working days of receipt of papers.
3. Cases where first letter sent to new client within 25 working days of receipt of papers.
4. Patients' statement of assets supplied within 10 working days of request or acknowledged within three working days and responded to fully within 20 working days.
5. Urgent payments dealt with within one working day of request.
6. Regular payments arranged within three working days of request.
7. Notifications sent to all parties within 15 working days of being informed of patient's death.
8. Statements of assets and liabilities prepared for the use of the Personal Representative within nine weeks of being informed of the death of the patient.
9. Grants returned to personal representatives within three working days of receipt.
10. Cases where assets released to personal representatives within six days of receipt of Grant of Probate or Letters of Administration.
11. Complaints to Heads of Division responded to within 15 working days.

Source: Public Trust Office

6.6 Performance against standards is reported to the Public Trust Office's Management Board and used for internal monitoring. Performance charts are displayed in the foyer of its headquarters but are not published more widely. Instead, the Public Trust Office publishes in its annual report a single key performance indicator measuring overall achievement against standards. Performance against this indicator has been slightly below target in each of the last three years. We consider that the use of an overall performance measure in this way is undesirable because it summarises performance across a range of indicators which are weighted by volume alone, although they are of differing importance to customers. Because the result is the sum of all items of activity, it is also disproportionately affected by indicators which have a high volume of transactions.

6.7 An alternative approach would be to publish individually the results for a small number of key standards which are particularly important to customers. The importance and greater visibility of the standards which customers most value would encourage the Public Trust Office to focus resources on the related activities. The remaining standards would continue to be monitored for internal purposes.

Recommendation 26

The Public Trust Office should use the results of its recent survey on standards of service to identify which of its Mental Health Sector standards are the most important to customers and publish performance against those standards in its annual report.

Information for prospective receivers

6.8 In 1994, the Public Trust Office was routinely sending receivers an appointment booklet which set out their powers and duties. We found that receivers would have liked more easily understandable information about their role. We recommended that existing guidance be expanded to provide further practical advice.

6.9 The Public Trust Office has since revised its general information booklet and has produced new material providing advice on making an application, information to nursing homes, hospitals and other carers, and about patients for whom the Public Trustee acts as receiver. It also provides a booklet on the duties of a receiver (Figure 7) which aims to raise awareness about the nature of the receiver's role.

6.10 Recent surveys of receivers conducted by the Public Trust Office have shown that more than 90 per cent of respondents felt that the information provided was relevant and clear, and that they knew where to go for advice. Organisations we consulted agreed that there had been improvements in this area; for example the Law Society, Alzheimer's Disease Society and the British Association of Social Workers praised the efforts that the Public Trust Office has made to improve and extend its range of publications.

Continuity of contact with receivers

6.11 Our 1994 report found that receivers and carers were dissatisfied with the frequent changes in the Public Trust Office's staff dealing with their case. Consultants commissioned in 1994 to examine business processes recommended that there should be a named, dedicated caseworker to deal with all aspects of each receivership, from the initial application to the termination of the receivership. The consultants considered that this would improve the quality of service to receivers and be more efficient, reducing the costs of appointing a receiver from around £270 to £120 per application.

6.12 Following pilots in 1996-97, the Public Trust Office adopted the consultants' recommendation: prospective receivers now deal with named caseworkers from the time they apply to the Court of Protection until the receivership is either rejected or terminated. The Public Trust Office believes that this change is improving efficiency, but that it is too early to say whether the projected savings will be realised.

6.13 The consultants also found that most of the staff they surveyed believed the structure of the Mental Health Sector of the Public Trust Office prevented them from effectively sharing experience in all aspects of customer service, and was not helpful in enabling them to respond to the needs of patients and receivers. They felt that increased teamwork would raise job satisfaction. The consultants recommended that the Public Trust Office should re-organise the Mental Health Sector to create a single Mental Health Division operating in casework teams. An important benefit would be to encourage closer working and skills transfer between staff working on private receiverships and Public Trustee receiverships.

6.14 The Public Trust Office set up a working party to consider this recommendation in November 1996. The working party, reporting in March 1997, did not fully accept the consultants' proposals. It made some recommendations for structural change but focused on merging non-casework functions of the two existing Divisions of the Mental Health Sector. Both Divisions have since introduced teamworking along the lines recommended by the working party. The Public Trust Office plans to consider more fundamental restructuring during 1998-99.

Providing a standard response to enquiries

6.15 In 1994, the consultants found that casework staff spent around a tenth of their time dealing with general enquiries, and that customers were often passed between staff before getting a satisfactory response. They recommended that the Public Trust Office should set up a customer services unit for the Mental Health Sector, and estimated that this could reduce by a third the time spent in handling queries.

6.16 The Public Trust Office accepted this recommendation and set up a customer services unit. In 1996, the unit's role was extended to external communications for the Public Trust Office as a whole. It is responsible for:

- providing clients with information in response to initial or general enquiries;

- obtaining feedback from clients on the service provided;

- publishing standards of service and reporting performance;

- assessing the impact of new legislation and practices on the Public Trust Office's work; and

- organising the work of the self-employed visitors.

6.17 The unit has seven staff. Each year they deal with around 60,000 requests for forms, booklets and other information. In 1995, the unit introduced a six-monthly newsletter to private receivers. The newsletter is aimed at non-professional receivers, and it is not sent to solicitors, who make up 13 per cent of all receivers. A web site has been set up on the Internet, and the Public Trust Office is developing a permanent policy on how to treat web site enquiries. The unit's staff give occasional presentations to external bodies, such as mental health charities and local authority social service departments, in order to increase awareness of the Public Trust Office's role, and in May 1998 they began providing training in receivership for local authorities.

6.18 A number of the organisations whom we consulted felt that the quality of service provided by the Public Trust Office had improved. For example, Rescare (the National Society for Mentally Handicapped People in Residential Care) told us there had been a noticeable improvement over recent years in the speed of response to receivers' enquiries.

Obtaining the views of clients

6.19 In 1994, we reported the results of our surveys of the views of receivers and carers on the quality of the Public Trust Office's service. In its subsequent report, the Committee of Public Accounts suggested that the Public Trust Office should undertake a follow-up survey. Since then the Public Trust Office has carried out five surveys to assess clients' general satisfaction and to obtain views on specific issues, such as the information provided to receivers and the operation of complaints procedures.

6.20 The surveys found generally high and rising levels of satisfaction with the service received, the helpfulness of staff and the clarity and relevance of information. Clients were less happy about some other aspects of the Public Trust Office's work, such as the level and calculation of fees and the way in which complaints were dealt with. The Public Trust Office has taken measures to improve quality of service on the basis of information provided by the surveys, although it has not yet established formal arrangements to monitor the impact of the changes it has made.

Recommendation 27

The Public Trust Office should produce action plans in response to survey recommendations and use them to monitor implementation and the impact of the changes made.

6.21 The surveys have so far all been postal questionnaires, focusing on quantitative data and suffering to some degree from low levels of response. The Public Trust Office is developing an external communications strategy aimed at obtaining more feedback on the services it provides and at publicising its services to appropriate audiences. As part of this, it is considering how to generate more qualitative information, for example by holding discussion groups for users.

Establishing more rigorous complaints procedures

6.22 Complaints are an important indicator of performance, particularly for organisations which deal extensively with members of the public. The Public Trust Office has widely publicised its complaints procedures and from May 1997 has also included an explanation of the procedures in its Charter Standards leaflet. The

Public Trust Office aims to use complaints as a means of monitoring and improving quality of service. Data on complaints are reported each quarter to the Management Board.

6.23 Complaints come mainly from receivers, relatives, carers and the patients themselves. In 1996-97, a total of 521 complaints were made to branch managers and more senior staff. The Public Trust Office does not monitor complaints made purely to caseworkers, though a 1996 survey of complainants found that 44 per cent had made their initial complaint to a caseworker. Since some of these may not be taken beyond the caseworker, the number of complaints actually received may therefore be higher than the reported figure.

6.24 In 1994-95 there were around 170 complaints and in 1995-96 some 330. However, data on complaints for years prior to 1996-97 are not strictly comparable, since in July 1996 the Public Trust Office extended the scope of its monitoring to complaints made to branch managers. Nevertheless, it recognises that the volume of complaints has increased over recent years, but believes that this is partly because users are more aware of their rights and are better informed about how to make a complaint. The Public Trust Office's standards (Figures 27 and 28) also help people to know the standard of service they can expect, and therefore whether they have grounds for a complaint.

6.25 Complaints generally relate to the level of fees, the operation of administrative procedures, and the quality of the service from Public Trust Office staff. Around 15 per cent of complaints relate to matters which are outside the control of the Public Trust Office, such as decisions made by the Court of Protection.

6.26 The Public Trust Office told us that it carefully investigates all complaints and, where the complaint is justified, it apologises. Where a patient's estate has suffered financial loss, proper restitution is made from public funds. Of the formal complaints made to the Mental Health Sector in 1995-96, a total of 234 (45 per cent) were considered to be justified, although client recompense occurred in only a small fraction of these. One of the Public Trust Office's published standards of service is to reply to complaints within 15 working days of receipt. It performs well against this target. During 1996-97, only seven of the 521 complaints received were not replied to within this timescale.

Enhancing the skills and expertise of staff

6.27 The staff of the Mental Health Sector of the Public Trust Office are recruited as general service staff and appointed to, and moved between, business units as required. They are not required to acquire professional or other qualifications, but do undertake internally provided training.

6.28 In 1996, the Public Trust Office carried out a training needs analysis based on workshops and staff questionnaires to identify individual training and development needs. This identified a need for training in legislative requirements and basic counselling skills, as well as other personal development needs. The analysis did not assess the professional skills necessary to enable the Public Trust Office to meet current and future business needs. There may, as a result, be gaps in the analysis relating to some areas of its business. For example, it has just three qualified investment managers. Junior staff in the Investment Division, which deals with investment decisions for Public Trustee receiverships (900 cases with a value of £102 million), have no job related qualifications and rely on in-house training. They have specified signing limits and refer matters to a senior accredited manager where the value of the transaction exceeds these. Two of the staff are studying for the Investment Advice Certificate on their own initiative but with financial assistance from the Public Trust Office.

6.29 The Government have set a target that all civil servants should be employed in organisations recognised as Investors in People by the year 2000. It normally takes organisations two to three years to obtain accreditation. The Public Trust Office began working towards certification in April 1996 and achieved it in December 1998.

Appendix 1: Recommendations

The Public Trust Office should:

Monitoring receivers

1   put in place procedures to ensure that late accounts are pursued vigorously by caseworkers with periodic mandatory review by line managers, and that it has up to date and accurate management information on the number and proportion of receivers with outstanding accounts and the action being taken;

2   in consultation with the Court of Protection, consider the need for enforceable sanctions against receivers who repeatedly fail to submit accounts promptly;

3   ensure that the level of insurance bonds of all patients are regularly reviewed and adjusted where necessary so that patients' incomes are adequately protected;

4   review private receivership accounts promptly so that effective and timely use can be made of the results of the review;

5   develop risk assessment of private receiverships to include factors such as the receiver's track record in meeting their responsibilities as a receiver, with a view to focusing on those receivers where patients' funds appear to be most at risk;

6   consider, with the Court of Protection, greater delegation of authority to low risk receivers;

7   review Public Trustee receiverships accounts promptly so that effective and timely use can be made of the results of the review.

8   The Lord Chancellor's Department and the Court of Protection should consider what safeguards should accompany the registration system for Enduring Powers of Attorney and the fees that would be necessary to fund such work.

Visitors

The Public Trust Office should:

9 publicly advertise visitor work, so that applicants with wider experience of dealing with people with mental incapacity are able to apply;

10 improve its monitoring of visits to Public Trustee receivership patients and ensure that visits are made to all patients each year unless, exceptionally, the patient's circumstances do not warrant a visit;

11 improve its management information on patients to be visited, the required frequency of visits, and actual visits made in order to provide assurance to management that visit requirements for individual patients are being met;

12 assess whether, for patients removed from the visit list, adequate trigger points exist to keep the position under review so that they are returned promptly to the list where changes in personal circumstances are such that visits should be resumed;

13 consider whether current arrangements for visiting are the most appropriate, or whether alternative arrangements, perhaps involving local organisations, with appropriate quality controls, or the appointment of additional visitors would enable more local delivery of visits;

14 monitor whether visitors are applying the guidance on repeat visits consistently;

15 improve and computerise its management information on visits to patients to ensure that visits are concentrated on patients with the greatest need and investigate the reasons for the wide differences in the visiting rates across regions;

16 ensure that visitors have up-to-date and adequate briefing on patients' circumstances to ensure patients receive maximum benefit from visits;

Managing patients' capital

17 ensure that there is a sufficiently robust system in place for monitoring panel brokers which would prompt early and effective action where there is evidence of poor performance;

Financial management

18 draw up an action plan to review all appropriate fee accounts, identify debts outstanding and establish material accruals, along with a timetable for the production of auditable accounts for 1998-99;

19 ensure that fee adjustments and errors in fee calculation are identified and are addressed promptly;

20 establish the correct fee position for debts and current fees for all cases and amend accounting records accordingly;

21 establish and implement a comprehensive income policy to cover the raising, recording, review and collection of fee income from receivership patients, with clear responsibilities for all stages in the process and appropriate management controls to monitor compliance with the policy;

22 introduce adequate procedures for identifying year end accruals and for applying the appropriate accounting treatment to all material transactions;

23 with the assistance of the Lord Chancellor's Department, ensure it has in place arrangements to provide independent validation of its efficiency savings;

24 differentiate costs and caseload data to a lower level so that efficiencies and inefficiencies of different types of work can be identified;

25 consider including in its Information Systems Strategy a time recording system that will allow it to cost accurately the time spent monitoring and administering receiverships;

Customer service

26 use the results of its recent survey on standards of service to identify which of its Mental Health Sector standards are the most important to customers and publish performance against those standards in its annual report;

27 produce action plans in response to survey recommendations and use them to monitor implementation and the impact of the changes made.

mittee of Public Accounts'	The main findings cf this National Audit Office examination	Reference
...are being used to pursue outstanding ...hip accounts awaiting review was cleared	Only 11 per cent of private receivership accounts are submitted on time and the Public Trust Office does not have satisfactory procedures to ensure receivers submit accounts or to ensure consistent adequate insurance cover for patients.	Part 2
...ounts have been set: ...eiver within eight weeks; ...our weeks. ...ure that reviews are kept up-to-date.	The backlog of un-reviewed Public Trustee receivership accounts has been cleared but the Public Trust Office has not met its targets for the timely review of Public Trustee receivership accounts (33 per cent against a target of 80 per cent). It has also missed the target for reviewing private receivership accounts (maximum of 34 per cent achieved against a target of 80 per cent). Because in some cases it was incorrectly recording the date when it received the receiver's account, the Public Trust Office reported internally that it had met the target in 46 per cent of cases raised.	Part 2
...ides who is to be visited and how often. ...visiting arrangements exist, no new ...quired. The Public Trust Office agreed the ...osts and protection for patients and was ...ffice stressed its responsibilities were	In summer 1998 the Public Trust Office asked the Court of Protection to revise the criteria governing visits to patients. The Court has now revised the criteria and the changes have been implemented. A slightly higher number of visits were undertaken in 1997-98 with 1992-93 (1,683 and 1,500 respectively) when the Committee considered the latter unacceptably low. The Public Trust Office believes the 750-800 annual visits of 1994-95 and 1995-96 were more typical years.	Part 3
...gements for visiting were not satisfactory ...and properly staff and trained section ...ice was to make recommendations to the ...such a section	The Public Trust Office took over responsibility for the visiting programme for private receivership patients from 1 April 1996. It appointed six self-employed visitors to carry out visits, for a flat rate of £65 per visit, a saving of over £140 per visit over the previous arrangements. There is a wide difference in the number of visits per 1,000 patients across the six visiting areas.	Part 3
...ons to review investment requirements ...circumstances. All funds where the ...managed by the Court's panel	The main performance targets for patients' investment portfolios have not been met. The contract of the under-performing broker has now been terminated.	Part 4
...those who benefit; (b) the taxpayer should ...) fees should be set having regard to ...y has proposed that more costs are	Since becoming an executive agency, the Public Trust Office has been unable to publish auditable financial statements. Weaknesses in accounting polices and procedures cast doubt on the reliability of published information on financial performance.	Part 5
...Public Trust Office. Target for the period of ...percentage recovery of Public Trustee ...e current level of 52 per cent to ...cases will be reduced and those for Public	The Court of Protection Rules 1994 increased the administration fees of Public Trustee receiverships while reducing the fees paid by most patients with private receiverships.	Part 5
	The Lord Chancellor has recently restated the policy that there should be no public subsidy for the work of the Public Trust Office. This has limited the scope for reducing the cross-subsidy. However the Public Trust Office has reduced the level of the cross-subsidy from 52 per cent to 37 per cent by 1996-97. In 1996-97 it fell further to 32 per cent.	Part 5
	The Public Trust Office has reported that it has met its efficiency savings targets since becoming an executive agency. Without audited accounts it is not possible to confirm that the targets were in fact met.	Part 5
...standards of services in the Public Trust ...ey to be completed by 31 March 1995.	The Public Trust Office has made considerable progress in improving its quality of service since 1994. It has established a Customer Service Unit to improve the way in which it deals with enquiries from the public, sought to ensure that as far as possible receivers deal with the same named caseworker throughout the receivership, introduced more rigorous procedures for responding to complainants and obtained the views of its clients on the quality of its service through surveys and by other means of contact. The changes have been recognised and welcomed by mental health interest groups.	Part 6
	The Public Trust Office met only ten of its 19 customer service targets in the Mental Health Sector in 1995-96, five of its 22 targets in 1996-97 and eight of the 22 targets in 1997-98.	Part 6
...ment an objective to provide sensitive and ...atements and will create a Customer ...es to full receivership.	The Public Trust Office has created a Customer Service Unit and undertaken several surveys of receivers to establish their views on service delivery. It has publicised customer complaints procedures. The Public Trust Office has not met its Charter Standards target since it was set in 1994. The Public Trust Office has continued to publicise Enduring Powers of Attorney as an alternative to receivership. Registrations of these have grown markedly in recent years.	Part 6

1994 Main conclusions and recommendations of the Committee of Public Accounts (1)	1994 Public Trust Office response to Com conclusions and recommendations

Monitoring receivers

1. The Committee looked to the Public Trust Office to ensure that in future all annual accounts would be submitted promptly and reviewed soon after they had been received.

The Committee conclusion was accepted. Computer accounts. The backlog of 887 Public Trustee receive by 30 September 1994.

2. The Committee were seriously concerned at delays in reviewing patients' accounts. The Committee found it particularly unsatisfactory that a large backlog of unreviewed accounts had built up where the Public Trustee was receiver, and noted that for private receivership accounts the Public Trust Office's rate of review deteriorated in 1993-94.

Following a review, increased targets for reviewing ac
- 80 per cent of accounts where Public Trustee is re
- 80 per cent of private receivership accounts within
Procedural improvements have been introduced to

Visiting patients

3. The Committee considered it unacceptable that so few private receivership patients were visited each year, and many not at all. The Public Trust Office should consider carefully whether it was achieving the right balance between cost and protection in its visiting arrangements for the vulnerable people entrusted into its care

The Court of Protection, not the Public Trust Offi The Master of the Court has directed that, while guidelines on categories of patients to be visite importance of striking the balance correctly be reviewing its existing arrangements. The Publi limited to the financial affairs of the patient.

4. The Committee did not believe that arrangements whereby visits were made by Lord Chancellor's Department Welfare staff were satisfactory or gave the task sufficient priority. The Department should come to an early decision on the proper locus of responsibility for the visiting function

The Department accepted that the administra and that patients would be best served by a d under Public Trust Office's control. The Public Tru Department by 31 March 1995 for the establishmen

Management of patient's capital

5. The Committee noted that Public Trust Office sought to tailor investment requirements to the needs of individual patients, and emphasised that these should be regularly reviewed, updated and subject to annual performance assessment.

Caseworkers have been reminded of standing instruc annually or whenever there is a change on the patient portfolio is greater than £100,000 or where the case is stockbrokers have an annual performance assessmen

Financial management

6. The Committee was concerned both by the high level of fees charged and the fact that private receivership patients were having to subsidise heavily those cases where the Public Trustee is receiver. It looked to the Public Trust Office to review and improve the financial management of its receivership work without reducing the quality of service provided to patients.

Fee policy is set so that (a) operations are financed by not subsidise the work of the Public Trust Office; and (ability to pay. A Public Trust Office review of fee polic recovered where the Public Trustee is receiver.

7. The Committee recommended that clear targets should be set for reducing the present cross-subsidisation between private and Public Trustee receivership and a firm action plan be drawn up. The Committee regarded it as unacceptable that private receivership patients should be obliged to pay for work that is nothing to do with them.

The Committee recommendation was accepted by the the Public Trust Office's Corporate Plan is to reduce th receivership cost from private receivership fees from 30 per cent by 1996-97. Fees for private receivership Trustee cases increased.

Customer service

8. The Committee noted that the surveys identified some areas of dissatisfaction and concern, particularly among lay receivers, and that the Public Trust Office proposed to implement a range of measures to improve communications, provide greater support and advice to its clients and publish standards of service.

The Committee conclusion was accepted.

Customer Care Unit to be set up along with published Office's Charter Statement.

9. The Committee looked to the Public Trust Office to examine the impact of these measures, perhaps by means of a follow-up survey.

The Public Trust Office was to conduct a follow-up sur

10. The Committee supported the Public Trust Office's work to make itself more accessible to patients, receivers and carers. The Committee also welcomed Public Trust Office's continuing efforts to publicise the alternatives to full receivership and encouraged them to pursue this with other bodies in the mental health field.

The Public Trust Office has included in its mission state responsive services for clients. It has issued Charter S Services Unit. It will continue to publicise the alternativ

1 Thirty-ninth report of the Committee of Public Accounts Session 1993-94

Appendix 2

A summary of action taken by the Public Trust Office in response to the concerns and recommendations of the Committee of Public Accounts

Appendix 3: Law Commission Report: Mental Incapacity

Summary of the observations and recommendations on the role and powers of the Court of Protection

Background

1   In April 1991, the Law Commission, with the approval of the Lord Chancellor, launched a review of the decision-making arrangements for mentally-incapacitated adults. The Commission had identified a growing concern about the: adequacy of these arrangements; gaps and uncertainties in the law; and the limited machinery available to protect incapacitated people from neglect or abuse. It noted a particular concern that people should be allowed, wherever possible, to make their own decisions, and that where intervention was necessary, it should be restricted to the person's needs and accord, as far as possible, with their wishes.

2   The Commission's report, "Mental Incapacity" (Law Com No 231) was published in 1995, and presents observations on existing arrangements, conclusions and recommendations for change. The review and recommendations were wide-ranging, covering all aspects of decision-making on behalf of the mentally incapacitated. This appendix summarises the Commission's observations and recommendations which are relevant to the current roles of the Court of Protection and the Public Trust Office.

3   The Law Commission noted the demographic context of its report to be one where a rising number of people are over 80 years old, living longer and therefore susceptible to dementia such as Alzheimer's disease. The Alzheimer's Disease society reports that there are approximately 670,000 people with dementia in the United Kingdom. That number is expected to rise as the population ages. Increasing home ownership by people over 65 is also expected to lead to a more widespread need for legal powers to administer what may be substantial financial affairs after the onset of mental incapacity. The Commission and the Law Society noted a growing concern about the potential for financial abuse of mentally incapacitated people.

Observations on the current role and jurisdiction of the Court of Protection

4 The Law Commission believes that the current jurisdiction of the Court of Protection is too limited in that it does not encompass decisions other than those of a financial or business nature. At the same time, the jurisdiction is too wide since it assumes that capacity is an all-or-nothing status, and does not allow for provision to be made for a partial intervention in a person's affairs, where there is a partial or fluctuating capacity.

5 The Law Commission notes a number of features of the current requirements of Court of Protection appointed receiverships, including: the requirement for full disclosure of all the patient's assets; the fact that control of any capital assets usually rests with the Public Trust Office; and that those to whom receivership powers are delegated must generally give security and submit detailed yearly accounts. It notes that the costs of this highly protective system of state supervision are charged to the patients.

6 The Law Commission was repeatedly told in consultation that many carers and disabled persons were anxious to avoid any involvement with the Court of Protection; that they were afraid of its costs and they did not understand its procedures, particularly the complex relationship between the Court and the Public Trust Office. Respondents to every one of the Commission's consultation papers complained about the Court of Protection's lack of a regional presence. The Commission noted that it was difficult to quantify how this affected those who might otherwise have recourse to the Court's jurisdiction, but it had no doubt that the present Court is perceived to be a remote and inaccessible institution.

Main proposals for change

7 The Law Commission proposed new legislation based on three principles:

■ that people are enabled and encouraged to take for themselves those decisions which they are able to take;

■ where it is necessary, in their own interests, that someone else should take decisions on their behalf, that the intervention should be as limited as possible and should be concerned to achieve what the person would have wanted; and

■ that proper safeguards should be provided against exploitation and neglect, and against physical, sexual, or psychological abuse.

The Commission proposed a new incapacity bill to bring under a single legislative umbrella all health, welfare and property decisions for people who lack mental capacity.

General authority to act reasonably

8 The Law Commission believes that there is and should be scope for some informal decision-making on behalf of the mentally incapacitated on personal, medical and financial matters, without certification, documentation or judicial determinations. It proposes a statutory provision to set appropriate limits to informal action, such that it should be lawful to do anything for the personal welfare or health care of a person who is, or is reasonably believed to be, without capacity in relation to the matter in question, so long as it is in all the circumstances reasonable for it to be done by the person who does it.

A release of payments scheme

9 The Law Commission believes there are many instances where access by a carer to a small sum of money owned by an individual with mental incapacity could be put to a very good use, but that this cannot currently be gained without undue delay and legal costs. The Commission recommended that there should be a statutory scheme enabling certain payments which would otherwise be made to a person without capacity to be made instead to a person acting on his or her behalf.

Continuing Powers of Attorney

10 The Law Commission recommended replacing the existing Enduring Power of Attorney with a Continuing Power of Attorney. This would differ from the present Enduring Power of Attorney as follows:

■ it would cover matters relating to the donor's personal welfare, health care, and property and affairs, rather than just the latter;

■ it could be registered at any time, even if the donor remains mentally capable;

■ it would not be necessary to inform relatives until after registration had taken place; and

■ registration would be a purely administrative matter to be undertaken by a 'registration authority'.

A new status and role for the Court of Protection

11 The Commission proposes a revamped Court of Protection with jurisdiction over health, welfare and property affairs. The Court would embrace the principle of variable capacity, i.e. decisions should only be made on a person's behalf where they lack the capacity to make that particular decision; and a person may regain capacity and therefore the right to make his or her own decisions. The Court would have jurisdiction to make certain decisions about medical treatment, and could pronounce on a person's capacity, and the scope and validity of their Continuing Powers of Attorney.

12 The proposed new Court would have a base in each judicial circuit. An appropriate number and range of judges would be nominated by the Lord Chancellor to exercise the jurisdiction of the Court, including district and circuit judges and judges from the Chancery and Family Divisions of the High Court. The range of judicial personnel available should enable cases, which vary in the subject matter and complexity, to be heard by a judge with appropriate experience and expertise.

13 The Law Commission recommends that the Court of Protection should be able to sit at any place in England and Wales as determined by the Lord Chancellor. The Court of Protection would retain a central office and registry to ensure the existing pool of expertise is retained

The handling of an incapacitated person's affairs

14 The Law Commission recommends repeal of the current legislation regarding the management of a person's financial affairs by a receiver or the Public Trustee. Managers would be appointed for an incapacitated person but they would operate under general presumptions that "single issue" orders by a court are preferable to the appointment of a manager. The manager should be given authority only over those areas where the person is incapable of making decisions; and that authority should be as limited in scope and duration as possible. The Public Trustee would continue to act as a manager of last resort.

Appendix 4: Study methodology

1   Our examination of the Public Trust Office focused on five key areas: the appointment and monitoring of receivers; visiting patients; the management of patients' capital; financial management and efficiency; and customer service. Evidence was collected in each of these areas as outlined below. We also interviewed the Master of the Court of Protection, and staff at the Public Trust Office and the Lord Chancellor's Department.

Monitoring receivers

2   We examined 113 private receivership cases out of a population of 19,500 active receiverships and 48 Public Trustee receiverships out of a population of 2,500 active cases. The sample was selected at random in June 1997 using the Public Trust Office's case recording system. The examination focused on the timeliness of the submission of accounts by receivers, the timeliness, completeness and extent of the Public Trust Office's review of the accounts and follow-up action, and the requirement for and adequacy of security bonds.

Visiting patients

3   We examined a sample of 50 visitor reports for evidence of the completeness and timeliness of visits to private receivership patients, the content and standard of reports and the action taken. The sample was selected as follows:

- 15 cases from our sample of private receivership reviews where the Court of Protection had commissioned a visit in 1996-97; and

- 35 private receivership cases selected at random from the case recording system.

4   We also reviewed our sample of 48 Public Trustee receiverships to consider the timing of the visits to patients and examined the timing of visits for a further 610 patients.

5   We wrote to all five current private receivership visitors to obtain information on how they make their visits and to seek their views on how the Public Trust Office manages them and how they consider the visiting of patients could be improved.

Managing patients' capital

6   We examined the adequacy of the Public Trust Office's review of portfolio performance through discussions with key personnel involved in the review process. We also examined 41 cases selected randomly from the 222 portfolios which had underperformed against the weighted index of stock-market measures by five per cent or more in 1996-97. Our sample covered the following areas:

- 30 cases managed by the two panel brokers;

- five cases managed by patients' own private brokers; and

- six Public Trustee receivership cases where investment decisions are taken by staff in the Public Trust Office's Investment Division.

7   The Public Trust Office could not directly assess the commission paid by patients to James Capel Investment Management in 1996-97 and 1997-98 in respect of the restructuring of portfolios, because it was not possible to differentiate between transactions which related to the restructuring and those which related to the ongoing management of portfolios (paragraph 4.32). We considered whether the commission could be assessed by comparison with the charges paid to the other panel broker, Capel-Cure Sharp, where there was no exceptional restructuring. After allowing for differential levels of activity, there was an overall difference of 38 per cent in commission charged to patients between the brokers, which would equate to an average of £450 for each of James Capel Investment Management's 750 patients over the two financial years 1996-98. This is equivalent to 0.075 per cent annually of the value of the average patient's portfolio (£300,000). However, we concluded that the cost difference could not simply be attributed to the restructuring alone, because the client bases may not have been fully comparable. Other exceptional activity or additional services provided, such as the work required when taking on new clients, could also have contributed to the differences in the brokers' charges.

Financial management at the Public Trust Office

8   To examine the accuracy of income, samples of 115 private receivership and 43 Public Trustee receivership cases were selected at random. Income due was calculated and the recording, invoicing and collection of this income was traced through Public Trust Office accounting systems. Systems for identifying year-end expenditure accruals were reviewed and all material amounts examined for the two months before, and one month after, the end of the 1996-97 financial year.

Customer service

9 We examined the adequacy of the Public Trust Office's existing customer service targets and standards, as well as performance achieved. We also examined findings from the Public Trust Office's surveys of clients and the action taken by the Public Trust Office to follow them up.

Interest groups

10 We invited comments from interest groups in the mental health field who had helped us with our previous examination of the Public Trust Office (HC 258 of Session 1993-94). In particular, we asked for their views on changes in the quality of service provided by the Public Trust Office since our previous report. The views of other relevant bodies were also sought. The groups were:

- Action on Elder Abuse

- Age Concern

- Alzheimer's Disease Society

- Association of Directors of Social Services

- British Association of Social Workers

- The Law Society

- MENCAP

- Mental After Care Association

- National Association for Mental Health (Mind)

- Psychiatric Rehabilitation Centre

■ The Relatives' Association

■ RESCARE: The National Society for Mentally Handicapped People in Residential Care

■ Royal College of Psychiatrists

■ Royal Society for Mentally Handicapped Children and Adults

We also invited comments on our report from the Public Trust Office's panel brokers, James Capel Investment Management and Capel-Cure Sharp.

11 The Association of Solicitor Investment Managers approached us towards the end of our fieldwork and asked to contribute to our understanding of the investment approach followed by the Public Trust Office and the Court of Protection. We welcomed their representations, while acknowledging that they represent commercial competitors of the panel brokers discussed in Part 4 of this report.

12 The Association told us that it believes remuneration of investment managers by an annual management fee to be preferable to the Public Trust Office's policy of remuneration on a commission only basis. This is because it considers remuneration by fees allies the investment manager's interests with those of the client by providing an incentive to maximise the value of the portfolio and, with it, the manager's fee; whereas remuneration by commission provides an incentive for the broker to deal. The Association also believes that the total level of remuneration received by the Public Trust Office's panel brokers is insufficient to enable the investment manager to devote adequate resources to the management of patients' portfolios and still show a reasonable profit. We considered this carefully. However, the Public Trust Office believes that the arrangements with the panel brokers provide good value for money for patients for the reasons given in paragraph 4.10. It is also clear from our analysis in Figure 21 that one of the panel brokers did perform relatively well in 1996-97 on a commission only basis; the relatively poor performance of the other panel broker is therefore unlikely to have been attributable solely to the method of remuneration.

Appendix 5: Timetable of events leading to termination of James Capel Investment Management's contract as a panel broker

This timetable summarises the main events leading to termination. There were other meetings and correspondence between the Public Trust Office and James Capel Investment Management (JCIM) over the period.

12 July 1995	Public Trust Office noted under-performance in capital terms in 1st quarter 1995-96 returns and analysed JCIM's largest holdings.
4 March 1996	Analysis showed 1-year capital target narrowly missed and 3-year target met by JCIM. Most under-performing portfolios were within 1 per cent of target.
25 March 1996	Honorary Investment Advisory Committee discussed JCIM contribution to the Public Trust Office missing the 1-year target. Performance monitoring confirmed.
4 July 1996	Honorary Investment Advisory Committee discussed 1995-96 outturn and 1st quarter 1996-97, noting rising number of JCIM portfolios failing 1- and 3-year targets, and what the Committee considered to be JCIM's slow reaction to expressions of concern. Agreed to discuss position with JCIM at next meeting of the Committee.
12 July 1996	Public Trust Office briefed JCIM verbally and in writing on the Committee's concern and actual performance.
19 September 1996	JCIM presentation to Honorary Investment Advisory Committee. Measures agreed aimed at improving the broker's performance against the capital targets. Public Trust Office wrote to JCIM setting out conditions for continuing with the contract to operate as a panel broker.
5 December 1996	Honorary Investment Advisory Committee meeting confirmed that JCIM should be allowed one year from September 1996 to improve its performance. Public Trust Office briefed JCIM and analysed restructuring of portfolios with the broker.
10 April 1997	Honorary Investment Advisory Committee reviewed 1996-97 performance. Proposed ultimatum to JCIM giving October 1997 as deadline for improvement in capital performance. Any decision to terminate the broker's contract would be made at the October meeting of the Committee.
18 April 1997	Public Trust Office briefed JCIM on the ultimatum but JCIM disclosed a computer problem which it believed had led to an understatement of its performance.
12 May 1997 and 5 June 1997	Meetings between Public Trust Office, JCIM and JCIM's auditors to discuss the computer problem.
10 July 1997	JCIM presentation to Honorary Investment Advisory Committee on investment performance and the computer problems.
9 October 1997	Honorary Investment Advisory Committee meeting reviewed performance and recommended the termination of JCIM's contract. Public Trust Office was left to give notice so as to minimise disruption to clients.
21 November 1997	Letter to JCIM from Public Trust Office Chief Executive giving notice to terminate the contract on 20 March 1998.

Glossary

Term in report	Explanation
Annual account	An account prepared by, or on behalf of, the receiver detailing what he or she has done with funds received on behalf of the patient, supported by bank/building society statements, receipts and vouchers.
Annual enquiry	A simple proforma statement from the receiver detailing what he or she has done with income received on behalf of the patient.
Attorney	The person holding and acting under the powers granted by an Enduring Power of Attorney.
Court of Protection (the Court)	An Office of the Supreme Court. Its function is to manage and administer the property and financial affairs of people who, through mental disorder, are incapable of managing their own financial affairs.
Donor	The person granting powers to another person under an Enduring Power of Attorney.
Enduring Power of Attorney (EPA)	A legal instrument by which an individual can grant a nominee authority to deal with their financial affairs in the event of their mental incapacity.
Honorary Investment Advisory Committee	A body of independent financial experts chosen by the Lord Chancellor, who give their services as advisers on a voluntary basis.
Investment requirement	A Court-approved specification of how the financial assets of a patient may be invested, for example to provide high income or long term capital growth.
James Capel Investment Management (JCIM)	Panel broker re-appointed by the Public Trust Office for four years in December 1994 and whose contract was terminated in March 1998.
Panel broker	One of two authorised investment brokers appointed by the Public Trust Office. It manages patients' portfolios, makes recommendations for transactions and executes the transactions after receiving the receiver's approval. It receives remuneration on a commission only basis.
Patient	An individual considered incapable of managing their financial affairs, as a consequence of medical disorder, by a qualified medical practitioner.
Private receiver	A person who is appointed in a private or professional capacity by the Court of Protection to administer a receivership. May also be a representative of a local authority.

Private receiver	A person who is appointed in a private or professional capacity by the Court of Protection to administer a receivership. May also be a representative of a local authority.
Public Trustee	Chief Executive of the Public Trust Office who also holds the statutory office of the Accountant General of the Supreme Court. In cases before the Court where there is no-one willing or able to act as a receiver, the Public Trustee will usually be appointed.
Public Trustee receivership	Receivership where staff of the Public Trust Office carry out the duties of a receiver on behalf of the Public Trustee.
Public Trust Office	The Public Trust Office came into being on 2 January 1987, and since July 1994 has been an executive agency of the Lord Chancellor's Department. It comprises a number of business areas which all deal with the management of the financial affairs of private individuals. This report concentrates on the activities of the Mental Health, Investment and Finance areas.
Receivership	A legal arrangement, made under the auspices of the Court of Protection, whereby an individual is appointed to manage the day to day financial affairs of a person with mental incapacity (a patient).
Special Account	An account managed by the National Debt Commissioners on behalf of the Public Trust Office which currently pays 8 per cent gross interest a year.

Reports by the Comptroller and Auditor General, Session 1998-99

The Comptroller and Auditor General has to date, in Session 1998-99, presented to the House of Commons the following reports under Section 9 of the National Audit Act, 1983:

Printed in the UK for The Stationery Office on behalf of the
Controller of Her Majesty's Stationery Office
Dd.5068630, 2/99, 5673, Job No. 72449